The Best of
KOOLER
DESIGN STUDIO
Cross Stitch Collections

Produced by: **Kooler Design Studio**
3527 Mt. Diablo Blvd. #256
Lafayette, CA 94549
kds@koolerdesign.com
www.koolerdesign.com

Kooler Design Studio Production Team
Creative Director: **Basha Kooler**
Editor, Book Designer: **Sandra Yarmolich**
Technical Editor: **Priscilla Timm**
Photographer: **Dianne Woods**
Proofreader: **Judy Swager**
Stitcher: **Chris Mitchell**

Published by: **Leisure Arts**
5701 Ranch Drive
Little Rock, AR 72223
www.leisurearts.com

Leisure Arts Staff
EDITORIAL
Editor-in-Chief: **Susan White Sullivan**
Cross Stitch Publications Director: **Cheryl Johnson**
Special Projects Director: **Susan Frantz Wiles**
Senior Prepress Director: **Mark Hawkins**
Art Publications Director: **Rhonda Shelby**
Imaging Technician: **Stephanie Johnson**
Prepress Technician: **Janie Marie Wright**
Publishing Systems Administrator: **Becky Riddle**
Mac Information Technology
Specialist: **Robert Young**

BUSINESS
President & Chief Executive Officer: **Rick Barton**
Vice President & Chief Operations
Officer: **Tom Siebenmorgen**
Vice President of Sales: **Mike Behar**
Director of Finance &
Administration: **Laticia Mull Dittrich**
National Sales Director: **Martha Adams**
Creative Services: **Chaska Lucas**
Information Technology Director: **Hermine Linz**
Controller: **Francis Caple**
Vice President, Operations: **Jim Dittrich**
Retail Customer Service Manager: **Stan Raynor**
Print Production Manager: **Fred F. Pruss**

Introduction

In 1985 Kooler Design Studio set up shop in the Diablo Valley of California. Over the years, Donna Kooler and her staff created a classic body of work for the needlework field that rivals any that exists today. Keen vision and entrepreneurial spirit have fostered a creative environment full of celebrations, milestones, teddy bears, laughter, and support, producing a stunning array of needlework designs that continue to inspire stitchers.

Through the doors of the studio many talented people have entered. Each and every one of the designers, photographers, editors, stylists, art directors, writers, and stitchers has contributed to the quality and success of the studio. Included in this diverse group are designers Linda Gillum, Barbara Baatz Hillman, Sandy Orton and Nancy Rossi. These four women developed hundreds of needlework and craft projects and became essential members of the Kooler Design team. When beginning the task of narrowing down the designs to include in this book, it became clear that focusing on the work of these four artists would best represent the style and personality of Kooler Design Studio.

The time has arrived for a renaissance of American cross stitch. Kooler Design Studio represents the best of the past, the present, and the future of needlework design. As we look forward to exploring innovations in needlework, join us in celebrating our classic, timeless designs.

I have had the honor of knowing and working with these artistic and inspired women, and it is my great pleasure to share with you the finest and *The Best of Kooler Design Studio.*

~ Basha Kooler

Library of Congress Control Number: 2011929068
"The Best of Kooler Design Studio" (ISBN 9781609003555).

PRINTED IN CHINA

Contents

A founding partner at Kooler Design Studio, Linda has a versatile style which includes compassionate wildlife, sunny samplers, and whimsical designs.

A self-taught artist known for wonderfully lush flowers, exuberant botanicals, and elegant angels, Barbara's glorious colors seem to burst from the page.

As a lifelong fan of classic embroidery, Sandy incorporates her affinity for traditional stitches and Victorian motifs into her historically correct and charmingly intricate samplers.

Nancy is a native New Englander whose love of fine art and wonderful sense of color, depth, and realism are all expressed in the verdant landscapes and breezy coastal scenes she creates.

General Instructions

WORKING WITH CHARTS

How To Read Charts: Each design is shown in chart form. Each symbol square on the charts represents one Cross Stitch. Half and Quarter stitches are represented by a smaller version of the symbol in the corners of the squares. The straight lines on the charts indicate either Backstitch or Straight Stitch. Colored dots represent French Knots.

Symbol Key: The symbol key indicates the color of floss to use for each stitch on the chart. Symbol key columns should be read vertically and horizontally to determine type of stitch and floss color. The following headings are given:

DMC — DMC color number
X — Cross Stitch
1/4 — Quarter Cross Stitch
1/2 — Half Cross Stitch
BS — Backstitch
Str — Straight Stitch
FK — French Knot
Cg — Couching

STITCHING TIPS

Preparing Fabric: Cut fabric desired size, allowing at least a 3" margin around the design. Overcast raw edges. It is better to waste a little fabric than to come up short after hours of stitching.

Working with Floss: To ensure smoother stitches, separate strands and realign them before threading the needle. Keep stitching tension consistent. Begin and end floss by running under several stitches on the back; never tie knots.

Dye Lot Variation: It is important to buy all of the floss you need to complete your project from the same dye lot. Although variations in color may be slight when flosses from two different dye lots are held together, the variation is usually apparent on a stitched piece.

Where to Start: The horizontal and vertical centers of each charted design are shown by arrows. You may start at any point on the charted design, but be sure to center the design on the fabric. Locate the center of the fabric by folding in half, top to bottom and then again left to right. On the charted design, count the number of squares (stitches) from the center of the chart to where you wish to start. Then from the fabric's center, find your starting point, counting out the same number of fabric threads (stitches).

HOW TO STITCH

Always work Cross Stitches, Quarter Stitches, and Half Cross Stitches first and then add the Backstitch, Straight Stitch, French Knots, Couching, and finally any beading.

Cross Stitch (X): A square filled with a symbol should be worked as a Cross Stitch, unless a Quarter or Half Cross Stitch is indicated in the color key. For horizontal rows, work stitches in two journeys (**Fig. 1**). For vertical rows, complete each stitch as shown (**Fig. 2**). When working over two fabric threads, work Cross Stitch as shown (**Fig. 3**).

Fig. 1

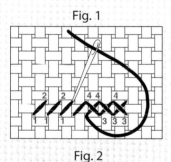

Fig. 2

Fig. 3

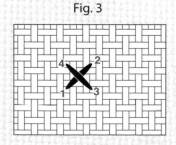

Quarter Stitch (¼): Come up at 1, then split fabric to go down at 2 (**Fig. 4**). When working over two fabric threads, work Quarter Stitches as shown (**Fig. 5**).

Fig. 4

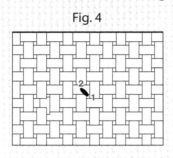

Fig. 5

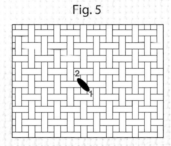

Half Cross Stitch (½): This stitch is one journey of the Cross Stitch and is worked from lower left to upper right as shown (**Fig. 6**). When working over two fabric threads, work Half Cross Stitch as shown (**Fig. 7**).

Fig. 6

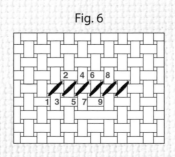

Fig. 7

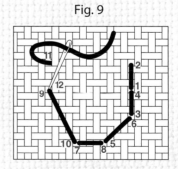

Backstitch (BS): For outlines and details, work Backstitch after completing the design (**Fig. 8**). When working over two fabric threads, work Backstitch as shown (**Fig. 9**).

Fig. 8

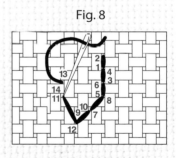

Fig. 9

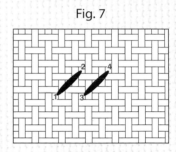

Straight Stitch (Str): For outline detail and decorations, work Straight Stitch after completing the design. Stitch with one strand of floss unless otherwise instructed. Bring needle up at one end of the stitch and down at the other end (**Fig. 10**).

Fig. 10

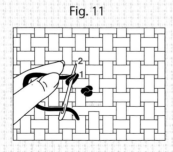

French Knot (FK): Work all French Knots after completing the design. Bring needle up at 1. Wrap floss once around needle. Insert needle at 2, tighten knot, and pull needle through fabric, holding floss until it must be released (**Fig. 11**). For a larger knot, use more floss strands and wrap only once.

Fig. 11

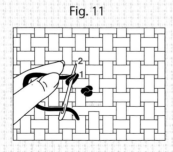

Couching Stitch (Cg): Use this to attach threads to the surface of the fabric using small, evenly spaced stitches. It is worked with at least two threads used separately. Fasten one or more threads at right end of line; bring it up to the top. Hold them in place along line with left thumb and attach them using tiny, evenly spaced stitches made with another thread. When a row is completed, take all threads behind and fasten (**Fig. 12**).

Fig. 12

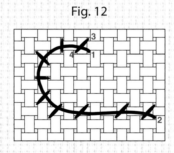

Beading: Beads add texture, dimension, and fine detail to designs. Add each bead with a stitch after all stitching is complete. Bring needle up at 1, through bead, and then down at 2. Bring needle up at 3, through bead again, and down at 4 (**Fig. 13**). Use floss to attach each bead where indicated on chart.

Fig. 13

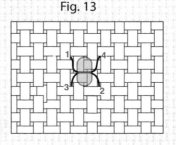

WORKING OVER TWO FABRIC THREADS

Use the sewing method instead of the stab method when working over two fabric threads. To use the sewing method, keep your stitching hand on the right side of fabric (instead of stabbing the fabric with the needle and taking your stitching hand to the back of the fabric to pick up the needle). With the sewing method, you take the needle down and up with one stroke instead of two. To add support to stitches, it is important that the first cross stitch is placed on the fabric with stitch 1–2 beginning and ending where a vertical fabric thread crosses over a horizontal fabric thread (**Fig. 14**). When the first stitch is in the correct position, the entire design will be placed properly, with vertical fabric threads supporting each stitch.

Fig. 14

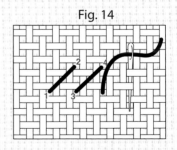

STITCHING YOUR DESIGN

Figuring the Size to Cut Fabric: Most projects include the size to cut fabric if you are making the project as shown in

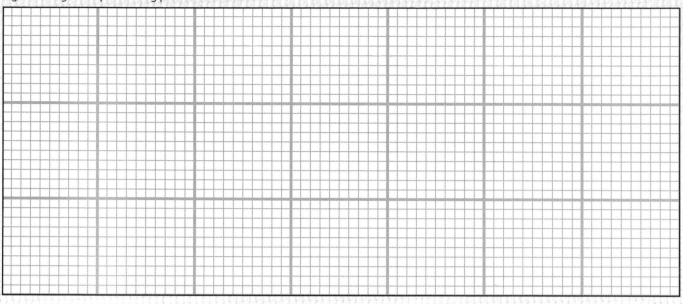

the photograph; however, you may wish to use a fabric with a different stitch count, or finish your design in another manner. To determine the size of fabric needed, follow the steps below.

1. Count the squares in the width of your design.

2. Divide that number by the thread count of your fabric. This gives you the width of your design in inches when stitched on the particular count fabric.

Examples:

70 squares wide ÷ 14 count Aida = 5" wide

70 squares wide ÷ 32 count linen worked over 2 threads (or 16) = 43/8" wide

3. Repeat the process to find the height of the design.

4. When cutting fabric, add at least 3" to each side of larger designs and at least 2" to smaller designs.

PERSONALIZING YOUR DESIGN

Cross Stitch designs that need to be personalized, like wedding or birth samplers, will have a "Personalization" line indicated on the chart. To personalize your design, use the alphabet provided on the design and the grid (**Fig. 15**) to determine the correct spacing.

BLENDING FILAMENT AND OTHER SPECIALTY THREADS

Blending filaments and other specialty threads may be combined with many other flosses and fibers to add extra flair to a design. Some of these flosses and fibers may also be used instead of six-strand embroidery floss. Special care should be taken when stitching with specialty flosses and fibers.

Use blending filament by itself or combine with other yarns to create random highlighting effects. Light Effects is a line of specialty threads that adds reflective qualities to needlework projects. The gorgeous shades include Precious Metals, Jewels, Antiques, and Pearlescent shades, plus trendy Fluorescents and Glow-in-the-Dark tones.

Blending filament and certain other synthetic threads are naturally slippery and require special handling. Whether you're stitching with several plies of blending filament or combining these specialty threads with stranded floss, you'll have an easier time if you tie the slippery thread to the needle. To use two strands of filament, cut a length twice as long as needed and fold it in half; insert the loop though the eye of the needle. Pull the loop over the

point of the needle, then tighten the loop at the end of the eye.

FINISHING BOOKMARKS

Mount your stitched bookmark on a piece of felt to frame it with color and give added stability. Cut the felt piece as instructed on the project page. Use an iron-on fusible backing to permanently bond the fabric to the felt (no sewing needed) and also keep the edges of your stitched design from raveling. For best results we recommend Thermo Web HeatnBond UltraHold which is available at your local fabric store. Follow manufacturer's instructions for permanent fusion, except do not prewash the fabric. Pre-heat a dry iron to silk setting. Place the fusible backing paper side up on the wrong side of the fabric. Glide the iron lightly over the paper for 1–2 seconds. Allow to cool. Cut around the bookmark as indicated by the cut line on the chart. Peel off the paper backing. With the adhesive side down, center the bookmark on your felt piece and iron for 4–8 seconds until bonded.

Linda Gillum

An honor Art School Graduate, Linda became a
founding member of Kooler Design Studio
in 1985 and has been an essential part of
the team throughout its history. Linda's
amazing artistic versatility is showcased
in her whimsical pets, charming
samplers, and sunny floral designs.
She is best known for her great
love and compassion for animals,
reflected in her vibrant wildlife
designs. Linda's family, her horse, cats
and Newfoundland dogs are her true
loves and passion, and this shines through
in her artwork. In addition to her renowned
needlework designs, Linda is also a fabulous fine
art painter and an award-winning doll maker.

Chapter 1

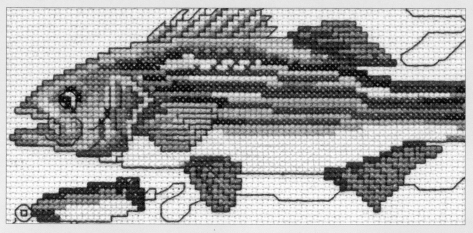

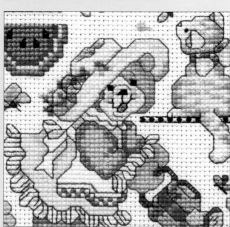

A Tale of
Three Fish

Design Information

Design stitched on 14-count natural Aida using 3 strands for Cross Stitch, 1 strand for Straight Stitch, and 1 strand for Backstitch.

Stitch Count

Each design is 106w X 52h in stitches.

Design Size

Each design is 7¾w X 4h inches on 14-count fabric.

Add 4–6 inches to each measurement for cut fabric size.

DMC	X	BS	Str	DMC	X	BS	Str
208	▲			726	◉		
209	α			762	⊘		
301	⊖			772	⊟		
310	■	✎		800	T		
351	⊕			809	△		
352	H			814	◆	✎	
400		✎		820	★	✎	
402	4			907	♣		
413	✕	✎		922			
435	✚			938	↑	✎	
437	L			951	I		
452	⊥			996	‡		
453	◇			3347	C		
469	◢			3348	▣		
472	Z			3607	↑		✎
666	♥			3765	V	✎	
699	✖	✎		Blanc	☐		
701	◈						

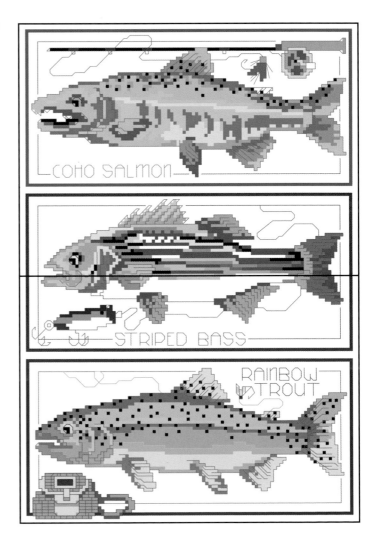

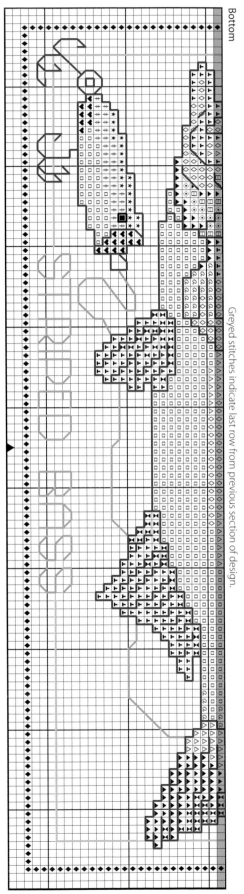

Greyed stitches indicate last row from previous section of design.

RAINBOW TROUT

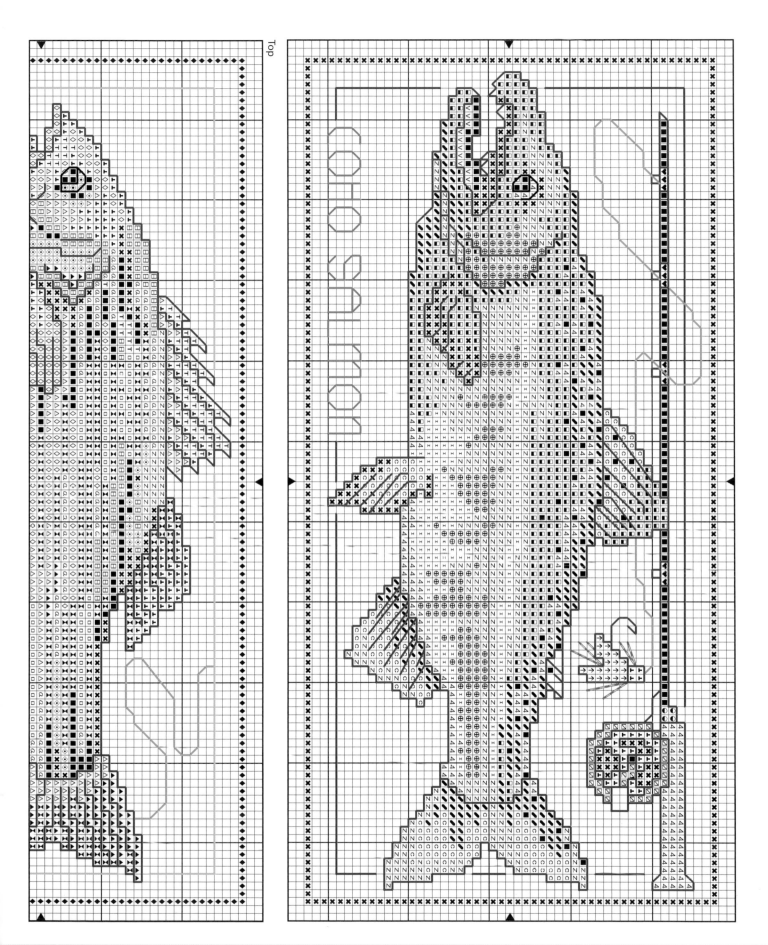

The Kiss
of the Sun

Design Information

Design stitched on 14-count white Aida using 3 strands for Cross Stitch, 1 & 2 strands for Backstitch, and 1 strand for French Knots.

Stitch Count

111w X 154h in stitches

Design Size

8⅛w X 11¼h inches on 14-count fabric

Add 4–6 inches to each measurement for cut fabric size.

DMC	X	BS	FK	DMC	X	BS	FK
310	■	◹		809	T		
561	◆	◹		820	◹		
666	♥			919	◖	◹	●
702	⊕			919*		◹	
743	⬆			922	□		
745	L			966	H		
798	⊙			970	✕		
801	✖			3341	△		

*Use two strands.

Top

Bottom

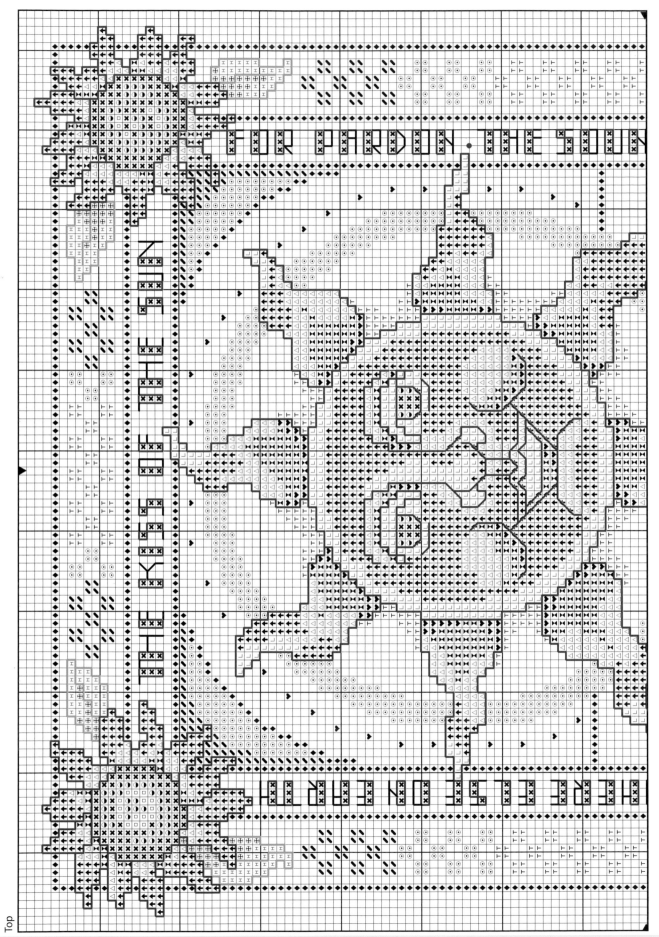

Bottom.

Bless the
Animals

Design Information
Design stitched on 14-count natural Aida using 3 strands for Full & ¼ Cross Stitch, 1 strand for Backstitch, and 1 strand for French Knots.

Stitch Count
160w X 216h in stitches

Design Size
11⅝ w X 15⅝h inches on 14-count fabric

Add 4–6 inches to each measurement for cut fabric size.

DMC	X	¼	BS	FK	DMC	X	¼	BS	FK
209	⊕	⊕			745	L	L		
301	▪	▪			762	V	v		
304	♥	♥			800	⊘	⊘		
310	■	■	▰	●	813	△	△		
318	⌧	⌧			826	●	●		
351	♣	♣			840	▐	▐		
402	✿	✿			841	↻	↻		
407	e	e			842	⊥	⊥		
413	◆	◆	▰		899	♡	♡		
415	⊘	⊘			950	◇	◇		
434	✖	✖	▰		986	◐	◐		▰
435	▲	▲			987	◑	◑		
436	✳	✳			989	#	#		
437	○	○			3024	✚	✚		
561	↑	↑	▰		3064	↓	↓		
632	▲	▲	▰	●	3326	4	4		
646	▱	▱			3348	⊥	⊥		
666	⊙	⊙			3772	▮	▮		
676	✖	✖			3776	◣	◣		
677	Z	z			3790				▰
703	♠	♠			3821	★	★		
738	∿	∿			3825	C	c		
739	H	H			3856	n	n		
741	2	2			Blanc	▫	▫		

Top left · Top right

Bottom left · Bottom right

Top left

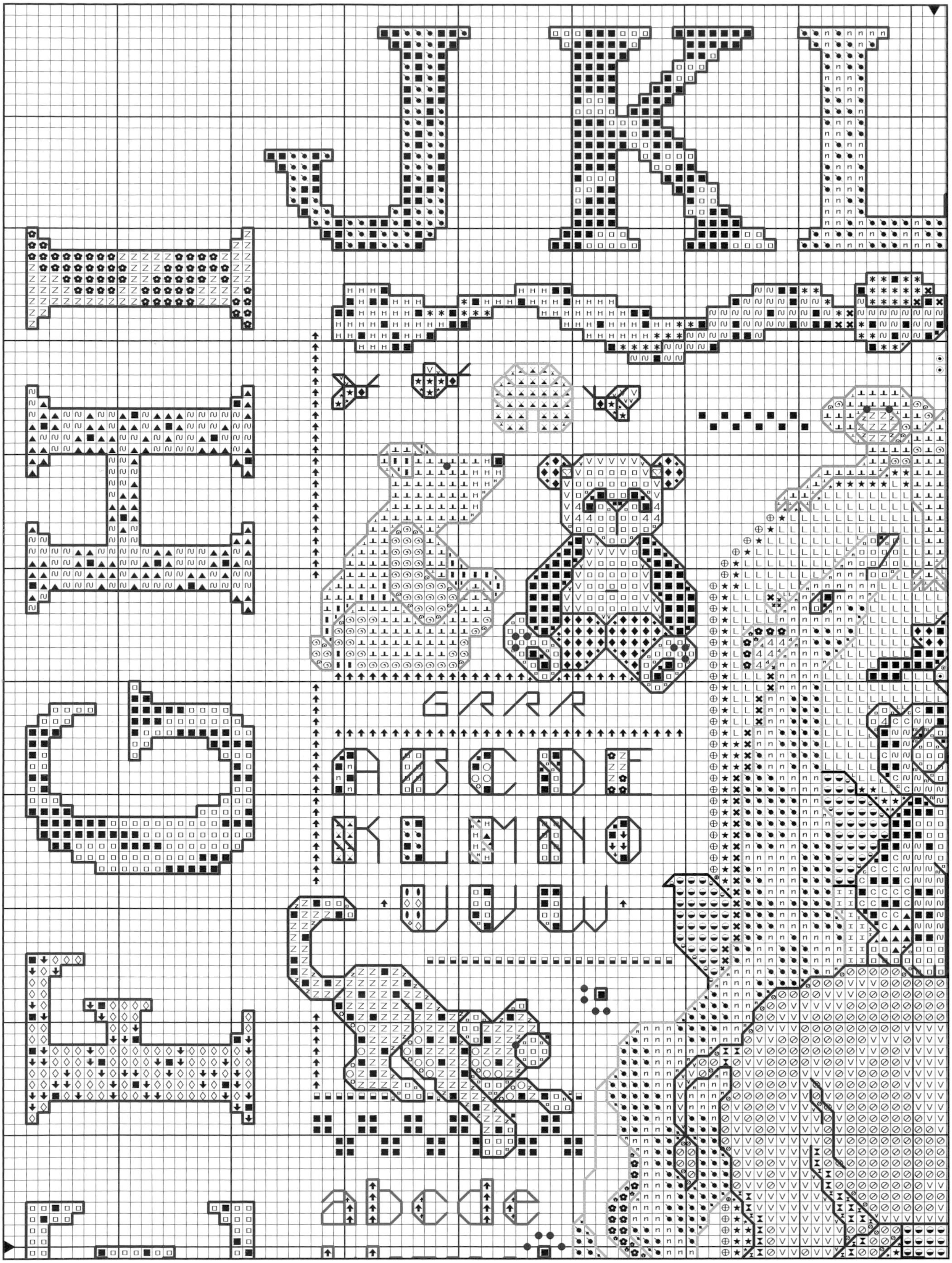

Greyed stitches indicate last row from previous section of design.

Greyed stitches indicate last row from previous section of design.

One Can Never Have
Too Many Cats

Design Information
Design stitched on 14-count white Aida using 3 strands for Cross Stitch and 1 strand for Backstitch.

Stitch Count
147w X 137h in stitches

Design Size
10¾w X 10h inches on 14-count fabric

Add 4–6 inches to each measurement for cut fabric size.

DMC	X	BS	DMC	X	BS
309	↓	▱	798	△	
310	■	▱	800	◇	
318	▱		824	↑	▱
351	⊕		898	⊠	▱
353	4		913	♣	
402	◓		920	▢	
407	H		922	⊥	
437	⊞		951	L	
562		▱	962	♥	
564	△		963	T	
632	✖		3755	+	
676	☆		3772	▲	
701	◆		3776	Z	
738	V		3799		▱
762	I		Blanc	□	
783	◣				

Top left   Top right

Bottom left   Bottom right

One can never have too many ~~~
:Ü: CATS :Ü:

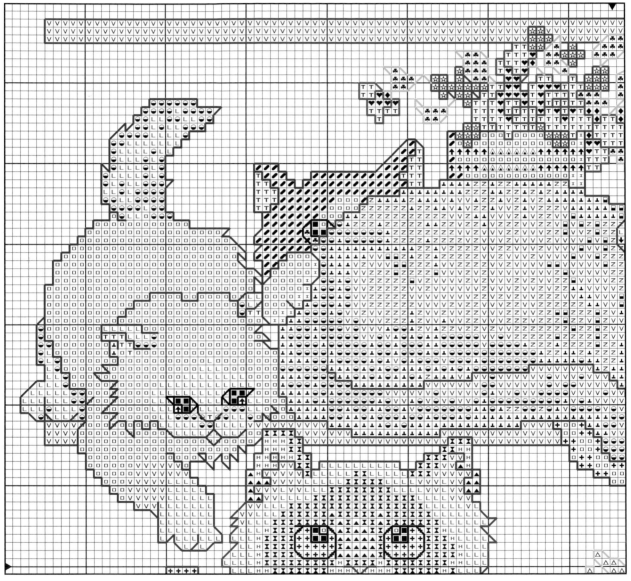

Greyed stitches indicate last row from previous section of design.

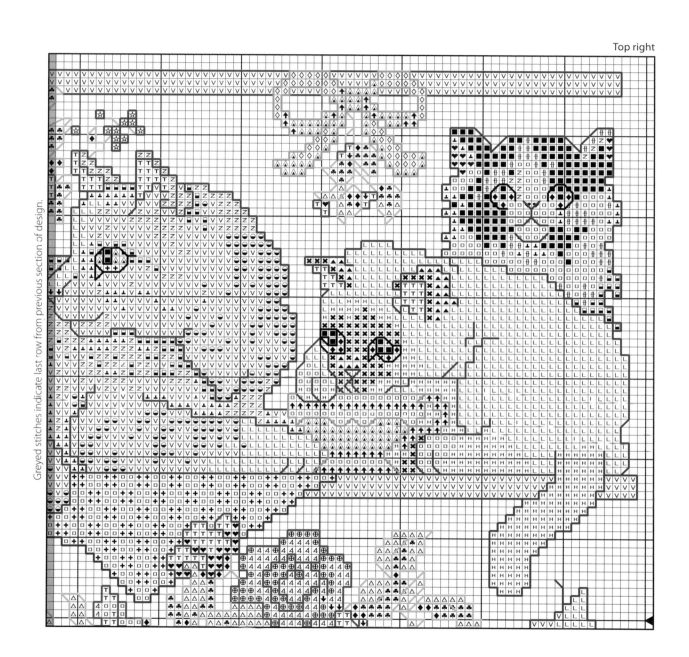

Bottom right

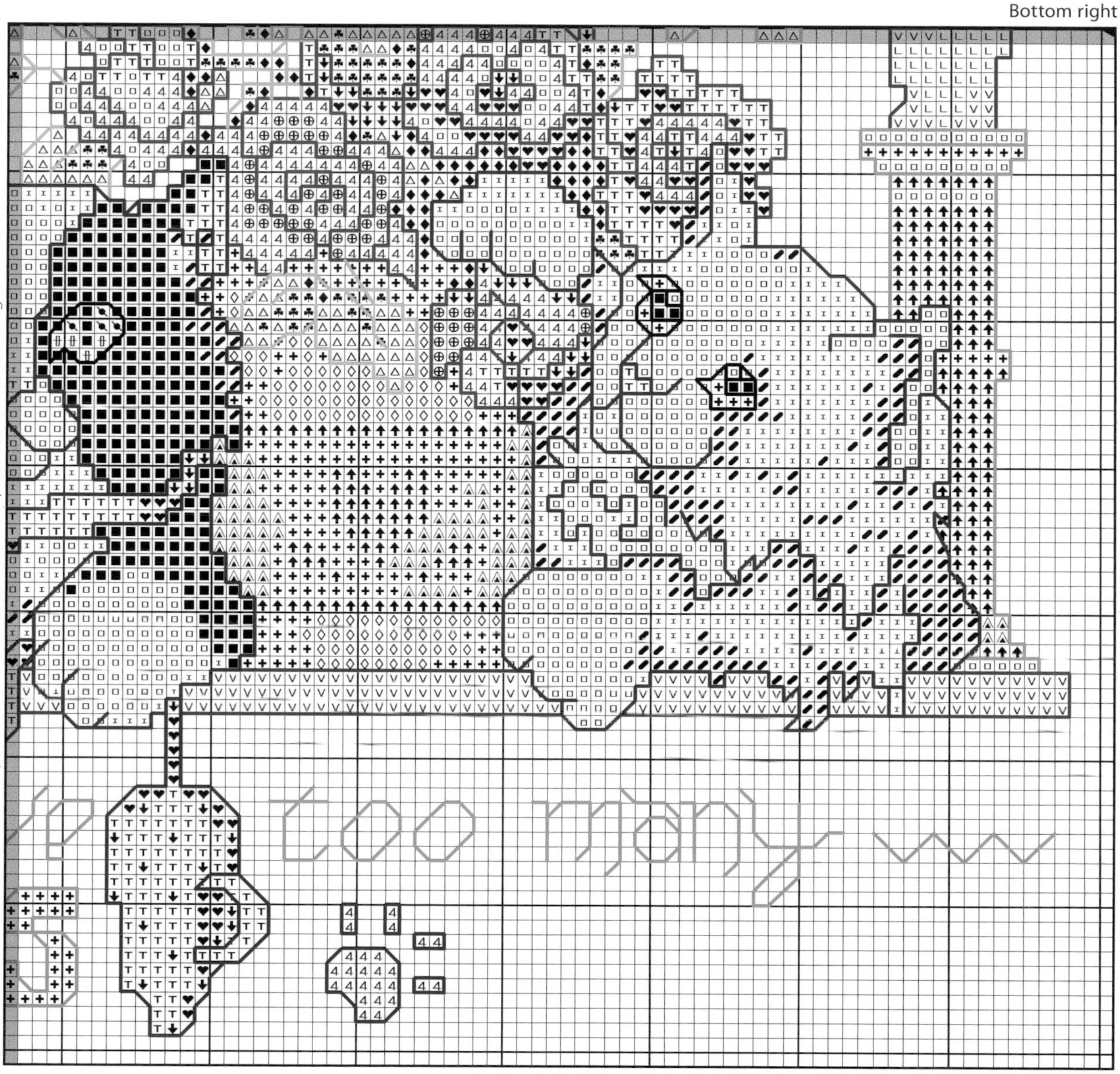

Greyed stitches indicate last row from previous section of design.

Yankee Doodle
Dandy

Design Information

Design stitched on 14-count white Aida using 3 strands for Full and ¼ Cross Stitch, 1 strand for Backstitch, and 1 strand for French Knots.

Stitch Count

153w X 165h in stitches

Design Size

11⅛w X 12h inches on 14-count fabric

Add 4–6 inches to each measurement for cut fabric size.

DMC	X	¼	BS	FK	DMC	X	¼	BS	FK
300					809	n	n		
310					814	♥			
318					816				
402		n			820				
413	◆				839	↑	↑		●
435	4				841	☆			
437					842	T	T		
666	⊕	⊕			921	✖	✖		
676	V				922	Z	z		
725					945	◇			
739	△	△			947				
762	I				3047				
775	L	L			3345	♣			
783	↓				3347	✖			
797	✖				3348	⊘			
798	⊞				Blanc	□	□		●

Top left

Top right

Bottom left

Bottom right

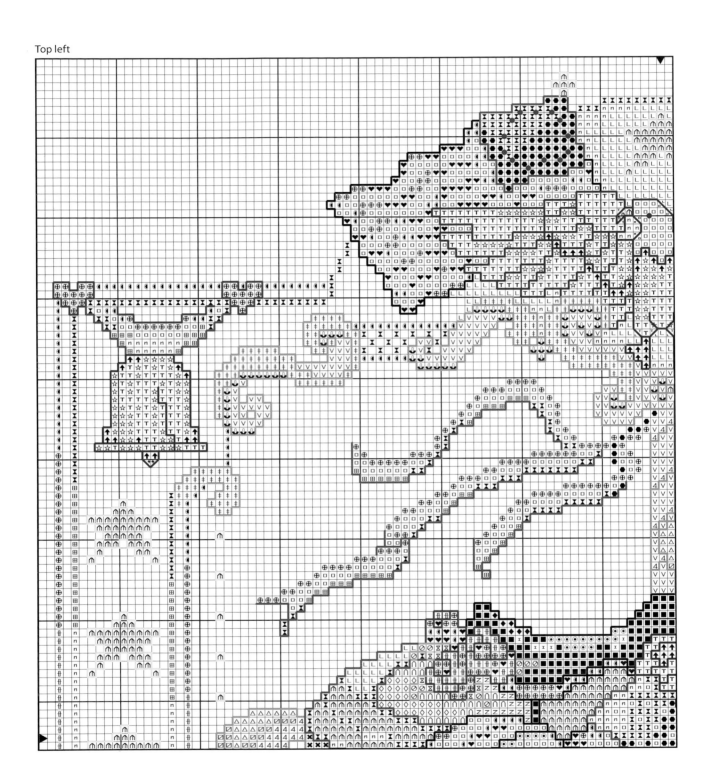

Greyed stitches indicate last row from previous section of design.

Bottom left

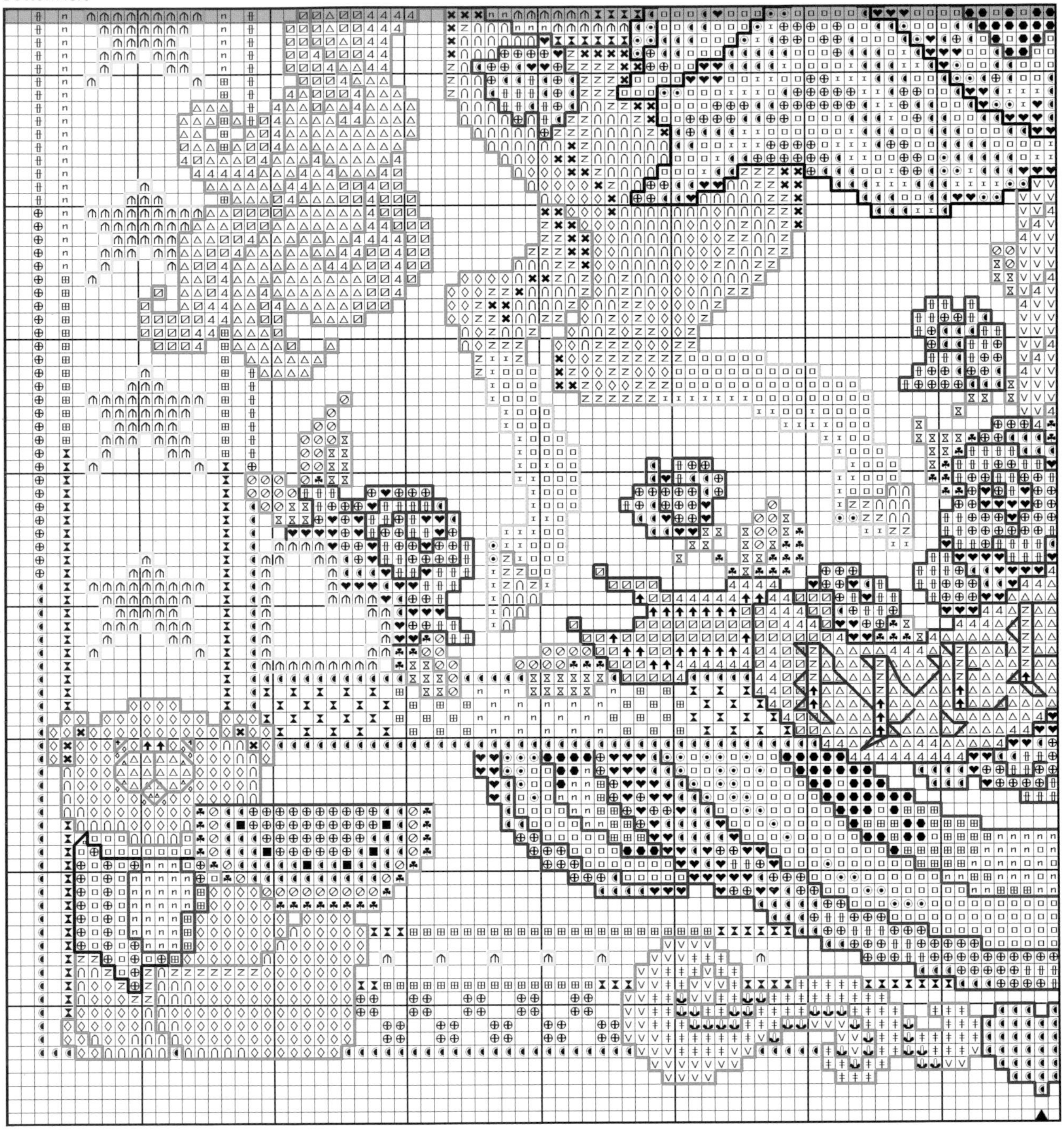

Greyed stitches indicate last row from previous section of design.

The Animals Came Two by Two

Design Information

Design stitched on 14-count antique white Aida using 3 strands for Cross Stitch, 1 strand for Backstitch, and 1 strand for French Knots.

Blends

2 strands 519 and 2 strands *014
2 strands 743 and 2 strands *091
2 strands 744 and 2 strands *091
2 strands 747 and 2 strands *014
2 strands 3810 and 2 strands *006
2 strands Blanc and 2 strands *032
*Kreinik Blending Filament

Stitch Count

180w X 195h in stitches

Design Size

12¾w X 13⅞h inches on 14-count fabric

Add 4–6 inches to each measurement for cut fabric size.

DMC	X	BS	FK		DMC	X	BS	FK
209	■				894	♡		
210	4				966	2		
211	∩				3024	L		
310	■	✎	●		3033	C		
317	⊥				3340	✚		
318	⊠				3713	○		
321	♥				3756	I		
353	⊕				3774	H		
402	⋔				3776	◬		
415	Z				3799	◆	✎	
422	7				3818	⊠	✎	
435	◖				3823	∩		
436	⊕				3826	✖		
437	⋈				3828	✕		
519	n				Blanc	□		
606	☆				519 / 014	◈		
640	✎				743 / 091	★		
642	●				744 / 091	✚		
666	⊙				747 / 014	⊕		
701	✚				3810 / 006	▼		
702	⊟				Blanc / 032	△		
738	V							
739	T							
744	a							
747	◇							
869	◣	✎						

Top left   Top right

Bottom left   Bottom right

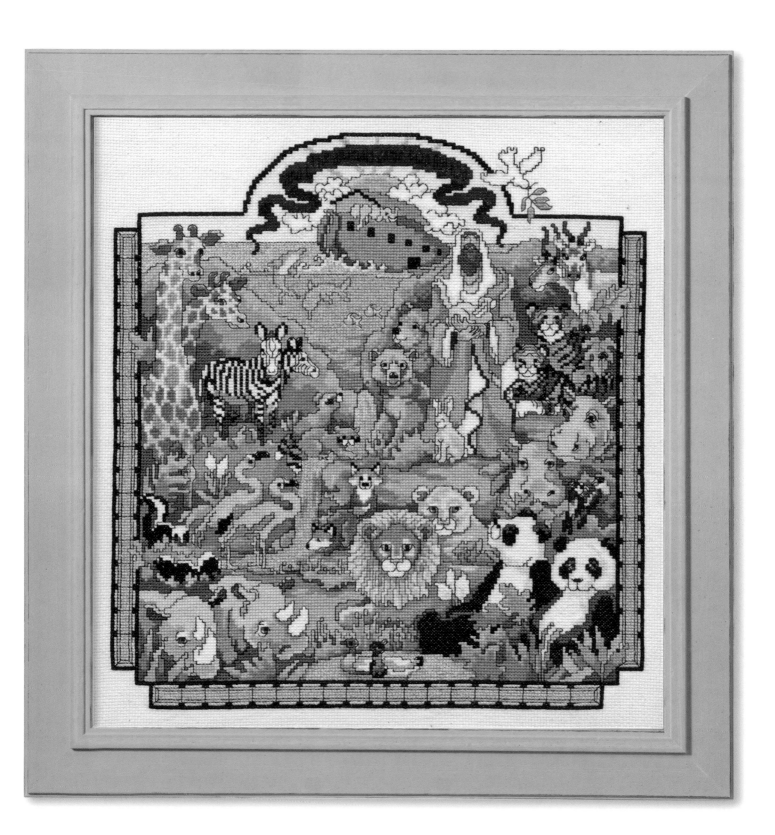

Top left

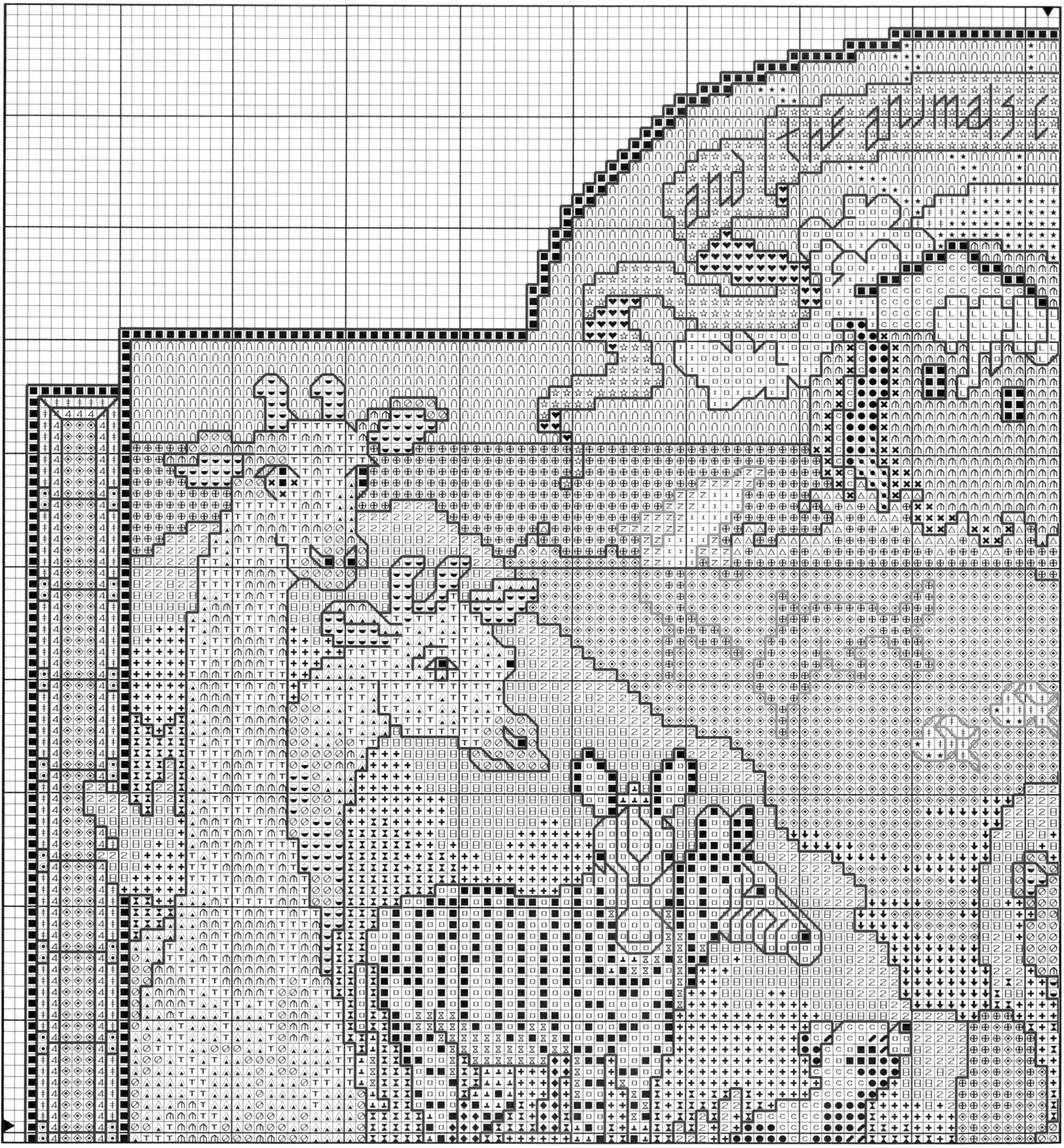

Top right

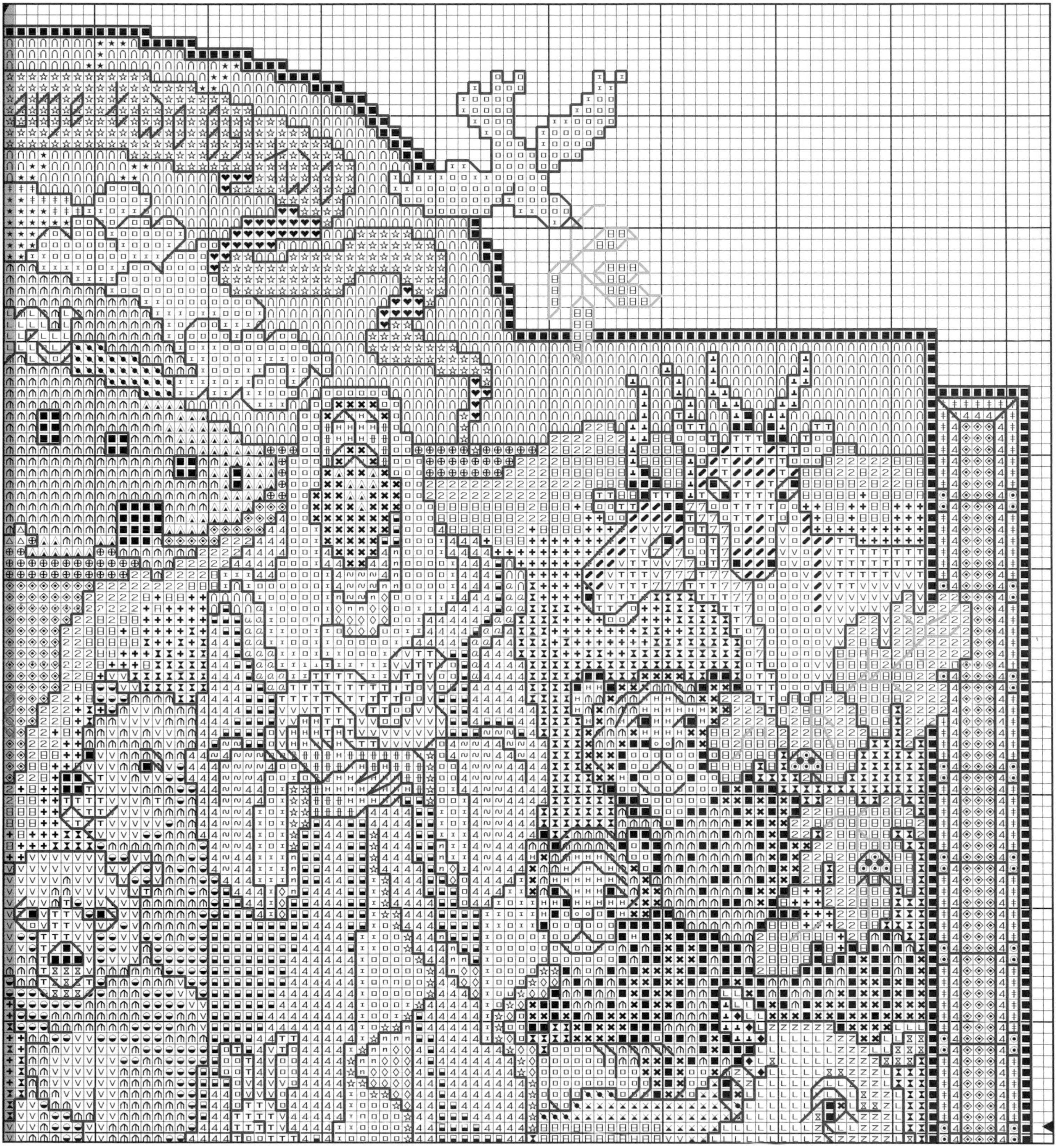

Greyed stitches indicate last row from previous section of design.

Willow Ware
Classic

Design Information
Design stitched on 14-count white Aida using 3 strands for Cross Stitch and 1 strand for Backstitch.

Stitch Count
141w X 182h in stitches

Design Size
10¼w X 13¼h inches on 14-count fabric

Add 4–6 inches to each measurement for cut fabric size.

DMC	X	BS	DMC	X	BS
221	◆		746	L	
334	◮	◢	772	T	
335	✕	◢	796	✖	
336	■	◢	798	★	
341	4		801	⬇	◢
352	C		899	♥	
402	⊥		951	⊕	
470	◉		963	I	
471	◇		3325	‡	
553	◈		3326	⋈	
554	⊞		3345	✚	◢
720	▣	◢	3609	∿	
721	◣		3756	△	
722	❭		3824	⋔	
743	●		3826	◢	
744	⁒		Blanc	▢	
745	Z				

Top left　　　　　　　　　　　　　　　　Top right

Bottom left　　　　　　　　　　　　　　Bottom right

Greyed stitches indicate last row from previous section of design.

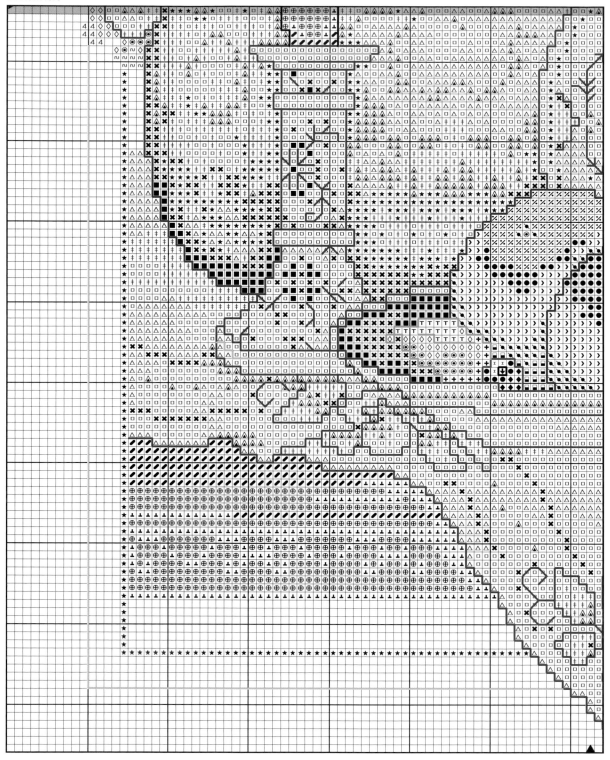

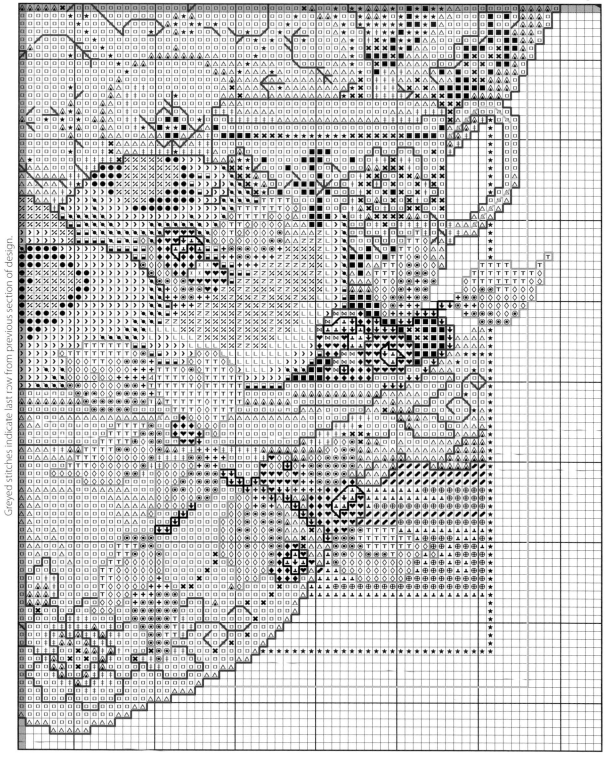

Greyed stitches indicate last row from previous section of design.

Summertime
Sampler

Design Information

Design stitched on 14-count White Aida using 3 strands for Full & ¼ Cross Stitch, 1 strand for Backstitch, and 1 strand for French Knots.

Blends

1 strand 744 and 2 strands 3348
3 strands Blanc and 2 strands *032
*Kreinik Blending Filament

Stitch Count

168w X 224h in stitches

Design Size

12¼w X 16¼h inches on 14-count fabric

Add 4–6 inches to each measurement for cut fabric size.

DMC	X	¼	BS	FK	DMC	X	¼	BS	FK
208	▣	◪			797	✖	✕	◣	●
210	◸	◸			826	♠	♠		
310	■	◪	◣	●	839	⊠	⊠	◣	
321	▮	▯			841	#	#		
402	m	m			842	4	4		
413	◆	◢	◣	●	899	✚	+		
415	Z	z			920	⊙	⊙	◣	
469	◤	◤			970	C	c		
606	♥	♥	◣	●	3326	◇	◇		
699	♣	♣	◣		3607	✚	✚		
701	✳	✳			3608	✳	✳		
704	n	n			3609	♡	♡		
722	⊞	⊞			3755	⚓	⚓	◣	
738	∧	∧			3761	△	△		
741	⬆	⬆			3770	T	T		
742	★	★			3776	◣	◣		
743	5	5			3856	◀	◀		
744	⋃	⋃			Blanc	□	□		
745	ⅈ	ⅈ			744 } 3348	a	a		
746	◦	◦							
754	L	L			Blanc } 032	✢	✢		
762	H	H							
772	V	V							

Top left / Top right

Bottom left / Bottom right

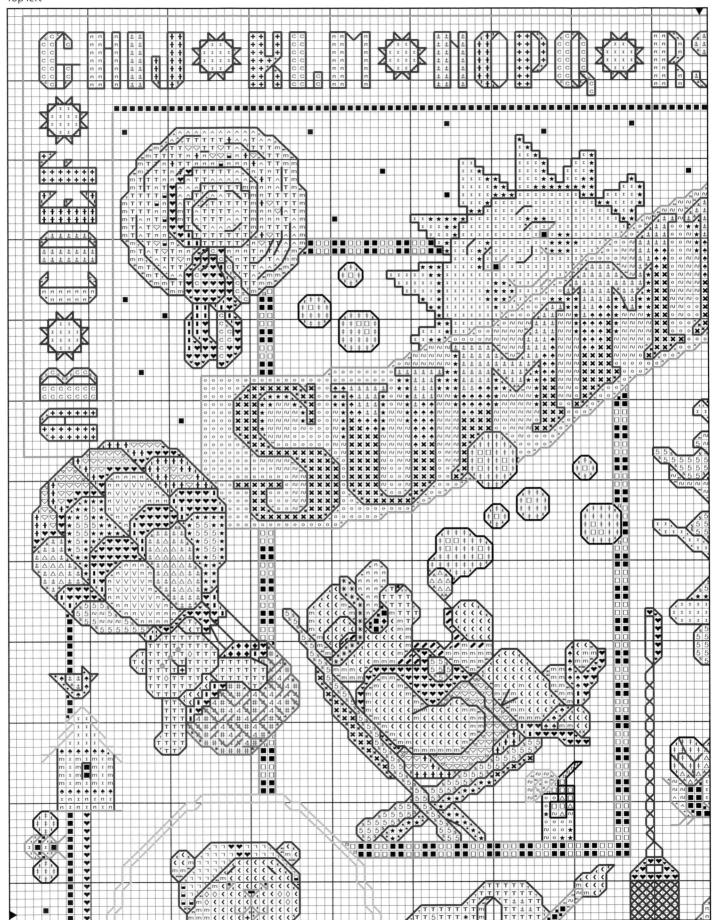

Top left

Greyed stitches indicate last row from previous section of design.

Barbara Baatz Hillman

People are surprised to hear that Barbara is a completely self-taught artist. She worked as a school secretary before 1991 when her natural talent as a painter led her to Kooler Design Studio, and she quickly became adept at needlework design. She finds peace in nature and is inspired by its colors. These influences are especially reflected in her gorgeous floral designs, which according to Barbara are 'simplicity stated.' Look for her signature dew drop on her bountiful flowers, since most of her vibrant designs contain at least one. Barbara's love of needlework has also taken her on a path to becoming an award-winning art quilter.

Chapter 2

A Perfect
Peony

Design Information

Design stitched on 14-count white Aida using 3 strands for Full and ¼ Cross Stitch and 1 strand for Backstitch.

Blend

1 strand 605 and 2 strands 818

Stitch Count

197w X 196h in stitches

Design Size

14¼w X 14¼h inches on 14-count fabric

Add 4–6 inches to each measurement for cut fabric size.

DMC	X	¼	BS		DMC	X	¼	BS
150	●	·	⬲		3 340	⋒		
304	♥		⬲		3341	⋁		
500	◆	◆	⬲		3345	⊥		⬲
561	✖	✖			3346	◉		
602	◣	·			3347	★		
604	△	△			3348	Z		
814	■	◪			3801	⬆		
890	▣				3804	⋒	⋒	⬲
894	4				3816	❯	❯	
935	◢				3824	⌐		
964	⊺	⊺			Blanc	▫		
3011	⧗		⬲		605 }			
3012	✚				818 }	T	⊤	
3013	⊞							

Top left   Top center   Top right

Bottom left   Bottom center   Bottom right

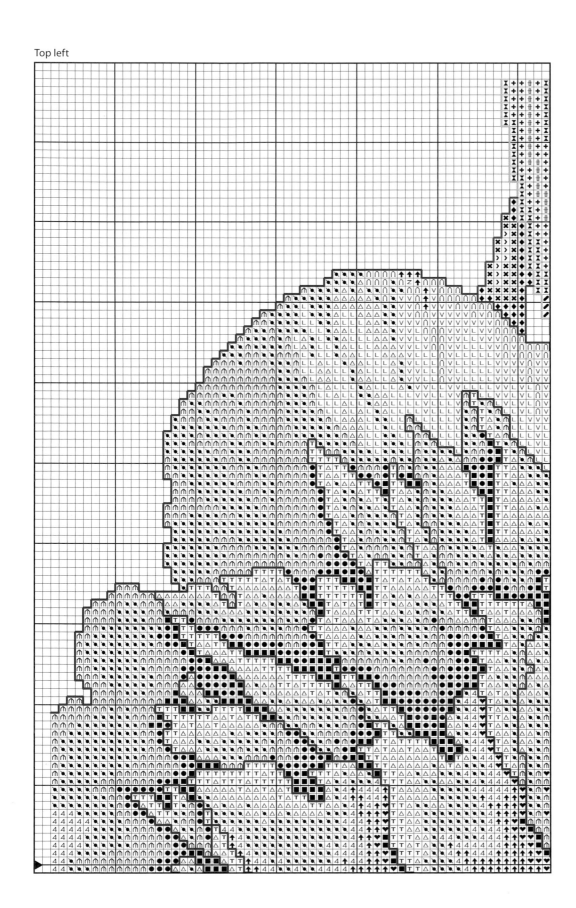

Greyed stitches indicate last row from previous section of design.

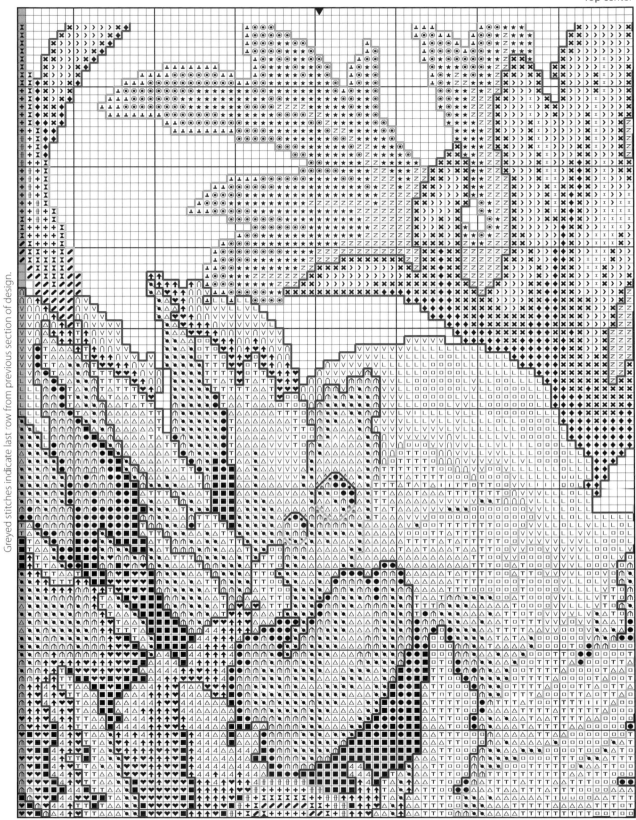

Greyed stitches indicate last row from previous section of design.

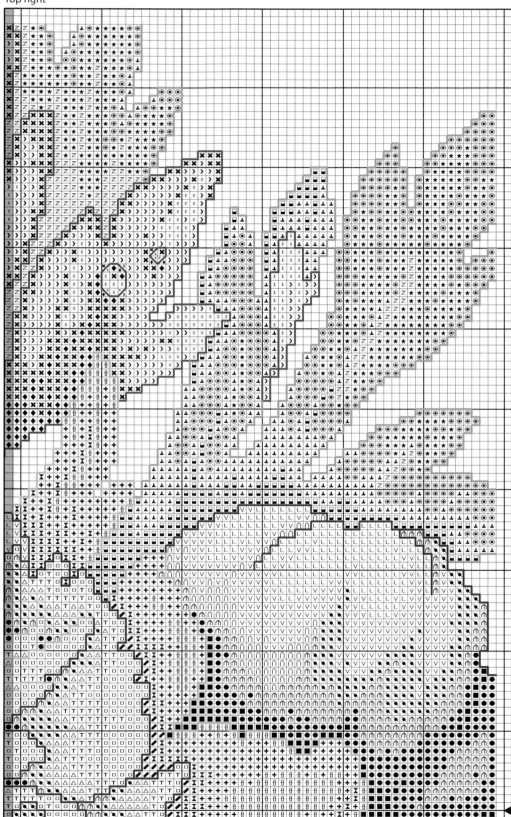

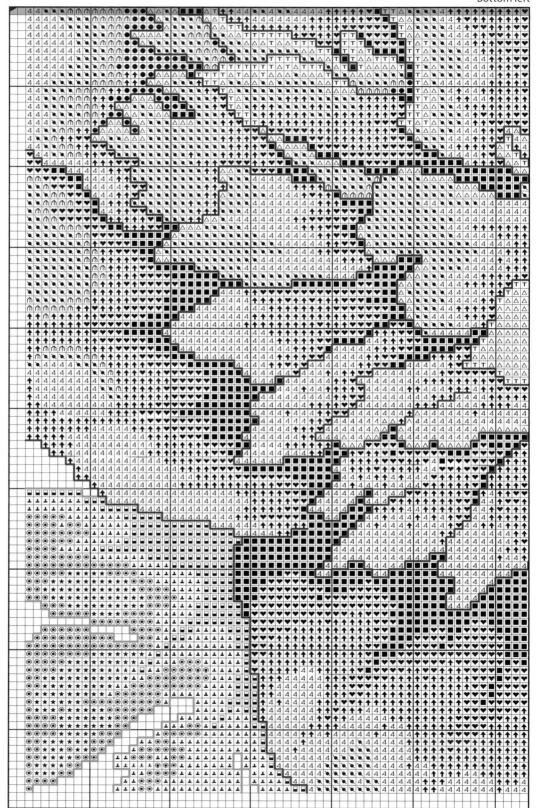

Bottom center

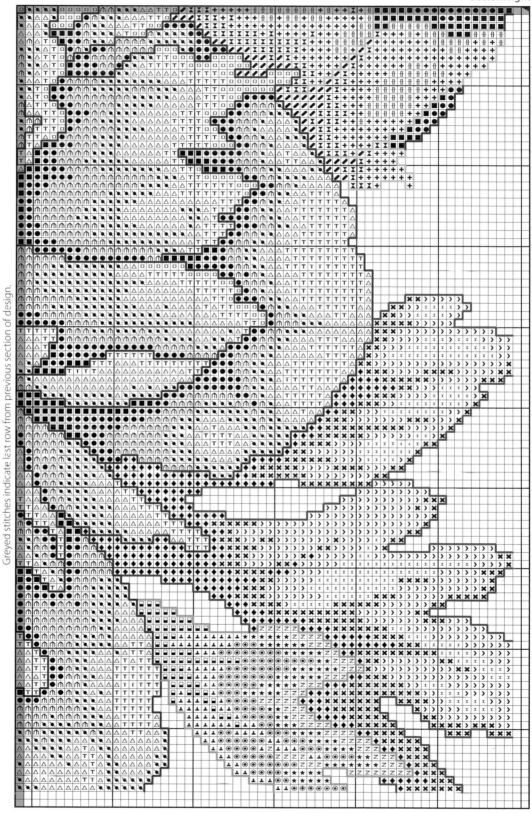

Greyed stitches indicate last row from previous section of design.

My Favorite Hat
Collection

Design Information

Design stitched on 14-count white Aida using 3 strands for Full and ¼ Cross Stitch and 1 strand for Backstitch.

Stitch Count

140w X 192h in stitches

Design Size

10¼w X 14h inches on 14-count fabric

Add 4–6 inches to each measurement for cut fabric size.

DMC	X	¼	BS	DMC	X	¼	BS
301				815	♥		♥
310	■	■		920	✖		
319	✕		⟋	922	4	4	
321				956	↓	↓	
322	✚	✚		959	Z	Z	
453	H	H		986	↑		
470	✕			988	L		
472				991	✚	✚	
535				3607			
605	C			3609	V		
647	∩	∩		3776	●	●	
722	✚	✚		3799			⟋
744	T			3801	◭		
747	⊥	⊥		3812	⋒		
772	◇			3827	⊘	⊘	
797	◆			3834	★		
800	△			Blanc	▢	▢	
813							

Top left · Top right

Bottom left · Bottom right

Greyed stitches incicate last row from previous section of design.

Greyed stitches indicate last row from previous section of design.

Spring Fever
Sampler

Design Information

Design stitched on 14-count ivory Aida using 3 strands for Full and ¼ Cross Stitch, 1 strand for Backstitch, and 1 strand for French Knots.

Stitch Count

169w X 225h in stitches

Design Size

12¼w X 16¼h inches on 14-count fabric

Add 4–6 inches to each measurement for cut fabric size.

DMC	X	¼	BS	FK	DMC	X	¼	BS	FK
210	◇	◇			824	◖	◖	/	
301	✚	✚	/	●	826	中	中		
309	▲	▲			894	∩	∩		
310	■	■	/		895	◓	◓	/	
317	⬆	⬆	/	●	915	◆	◆	/	
318	⊕	⊕			963	H	H		
351	$	$			986	⧗			
352	I	I			987	%	%		
400	◣	◣			989	7	7		
543	⟩	⟩			3348	△	△		
553	⊥	⊥			3607	✖	✖		
718	◤				3609	4	4		
720	▣	▣			3761	C	C		
741	◀	◀			3776	◉	◉		
742	★				3813	●	●		
745	T	T			3816	◩	◩		
747	L	L			3827	a	a		
762	◗	◗			3855	Z	Z		
813	⋈	⋈			3863	◈	◈		
816	♥	♥			3864	∩	∩		
818	V	V			Blanc	□	□		

Top left · Top right

Bottom left · Bottom right

APRIL SHOWERS BRING MAY FLOWERS

APRIL SHOWERS BRING MAY FLOWERS

Greyed stitches indicate last row from previous section of design.

Celtic
Angel

Design Information

Design stitched on 28-count antique white Monaco Evenweave over 2 threads using 3 strands for Cross Stitch, 1 strand for Straight Stitch, 1 & 2 strands for Backstitch, and 1 strand for Couching.

Blends

1 strand 452 and 2 strands 453

1 strand 453, 2 strands 452, and 2 strands *032

1 strand 726 and 2 strands 743

1 strand 946 and 2 strands 970

3 strands Blanc and 1 strand *032

1 strand Blanc and 2 strands 453

1 strand Blanc, 2 strands 453, and 2 strands *032

* Kreinik Blending Filament

Specialty Stitches

1 strand **E3852 Gold for Straight Stitch and Backstitch

2 strands **E3852 Gold for Couching

1 strand **E699 Green Emerald for Backstitch

02011† Mill Hill Seed Beads Victorian Gold

** DMC Light Effects

Stitch Count

188w X 223h in stitches

Design Size

13⅝w X 16⅛h inches on 14-count fabric

Add 4–6 inches to each measurement for cut fabric size.

DMC	X	BS	Str	Cg	DMC	X	BS	Str	Cg
211	△				3348	e			
310	■				3609	L			
353	V				3776	♡			
451		◢			3818	◣		◢	
517	⬆				Blanc	▢			
550		◢			452 453	⊙			
553	⊕				453 452 032	Z			
564	4								
700	◖				726 743	★			
701	⋒								
703	7				946 970	⊥			
741	2				Blanc 032	○			
754	⊥								
813	◑				Blanc 453	H			
827	T								
838	◆	◢			Blanc 453 032	⋒			
890	✖	◢							
913	◇				02011†	●			
920	✚		◢		E3852	C	◢	◢	
943	▣				E3852				◢
958	✝				E699			◢	
961			◢						
963	⊞								
964	❭								

Top left   Top center   Top right

Bottom left   Bottom center   Bottom right

Top left

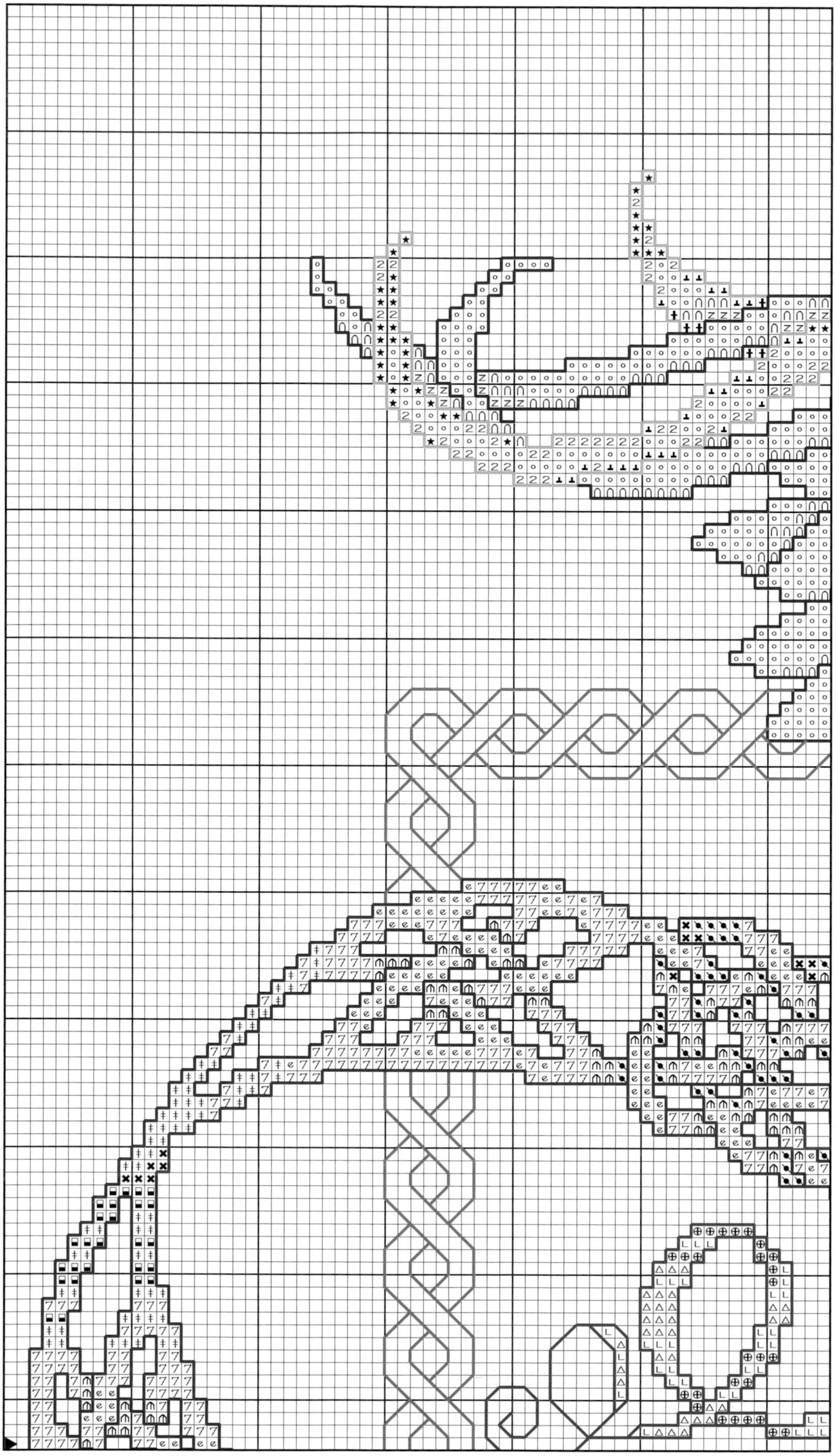

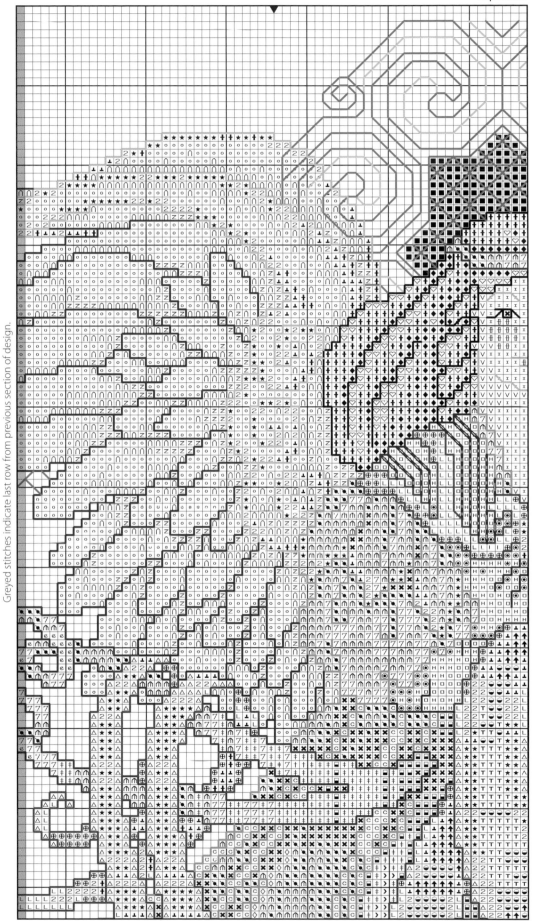

Greyed stitches indicate last row from previous section of design.

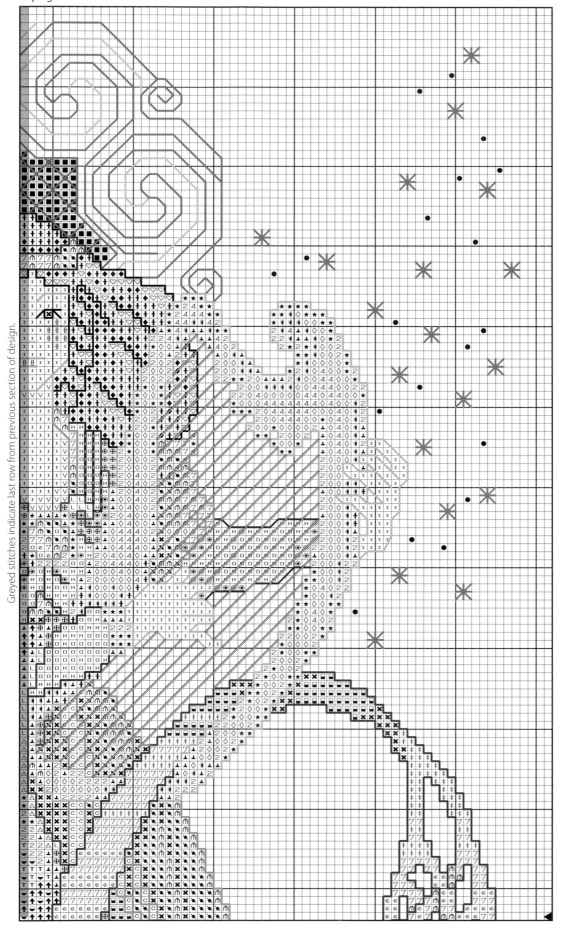

Greyed stitches indicate last row from previous section of design.

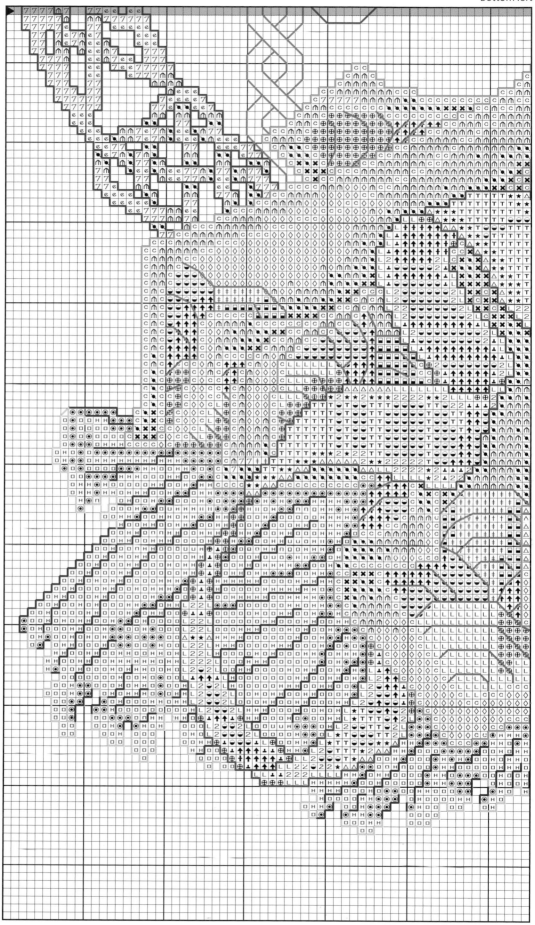

Bottom center

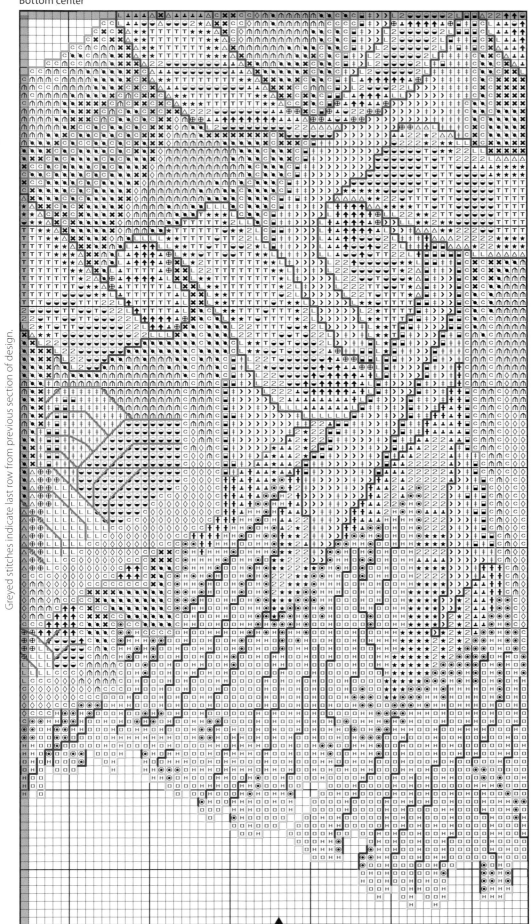

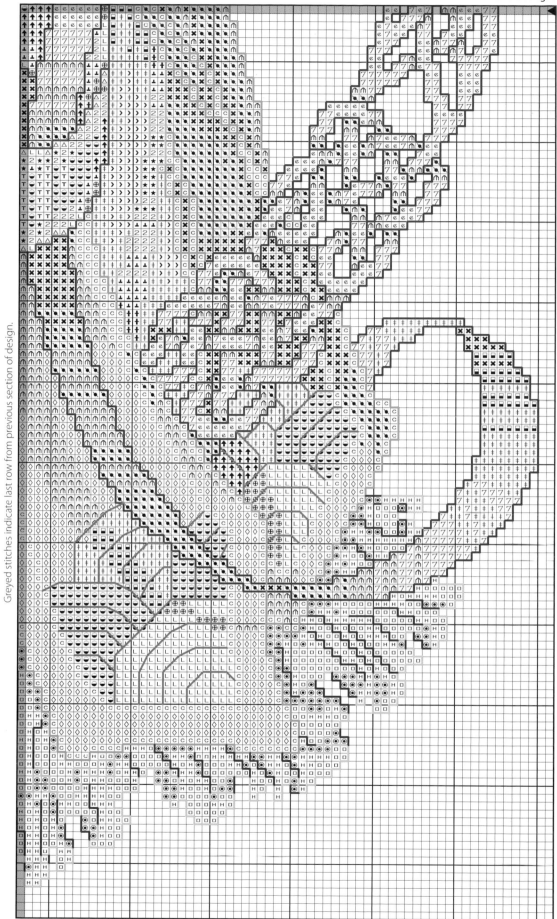

Greyed stitches indicate last row from previous section of design.

Barbara Baatz Hillman

Crate Labels:
Carrots

Design Information

Design stitched on 28-count tea-dyed linen over 2 threads using 3 strands for Cross Stitch and 1 strand for Backstitch.

Blends

1 strand 606 and 2 strands 918

1 strand 958 and 2 strands 3816

1 strand 964 and 2 strands 3816

1 strand 907 and 2 strands 3348

Stitch Count

90w X 80h in stitches

Design Size

6⅝w X 6h inches on 28-count fabric

Add 4–6 inches to each measurement for cut fabric size.

DMC	X	BS		DMC	X	BS		DMC	X	BS
310	■	◗		905	✖			606 }918	♥	
606	⋔	◗		946	⊙			958 }3816	⬆	
742	★			970	◪					
745	L	◗		995		◗		964 }3816	H	
772	T			996	⊥					
801	⊠	◗		Blanc	▢			907 }3348	Z	
895	◆	◗								

Barbara Baatz Hillman

Crate Labels:
Lemons

Design Information

Design stitched on 28-count tea-dyed linen over 2 threads using 3 strands for Cross Stitch and 1 strand for Backstitch.

Blends

1 strand 985 and 2 strands 939
1 strand 907 and 2 strands 3348

Stitch Count

90w X 82h in stitches

Design Size

6⅝w X 6⅛h inches on 28-count fabric

Add 4–6 inches to each measurement for cut fabric size.

DMC	X	BS	DMC	X	BS	DMC	X	BS
209	+		783	♥		3013	◇	
307	⋔		798	⊥	⟋	3753	⋂	
310	■	⟋	809	⋈		3813	❯	
400		⟋	820	✖		3816	▣	
444	Ⅰ		838		⟋	3826	✚	
501	◣	⟋	895		⟋	Blanc	▢	
730	⬆		905	Z		895 ⎫ 939 ⎭	⊠	
742	★		986	⟋				
745	L		3011	◆	⟋	907 ⎫ 3348 ⎭	△	
772	H		3012	◖				

Barbara Baatz Hillman

Crate Labels:
Tomatoes

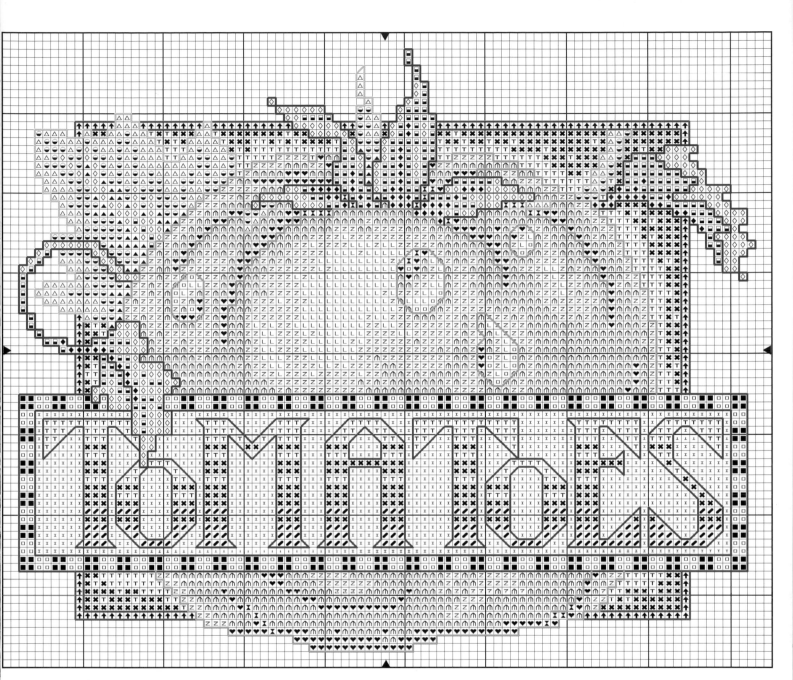

Design Information

Design stitched on 28-count white linen over 2 threads using 3 strands for Cross Stitch and 1 strand for Backstitch.

Blends

1 strand 321 and 2 strands 498
1 strand 922 and 2 strands 977
1 strand 958 and 2 strands 3816
1 strand 964 and 2 strands 3813

Stitch Count

91w X 75h in stitches

Design Size

6¾w X 5⅝h inches on 28-count fabric

Add 4–6 inches to each measurement for cut fabric size.

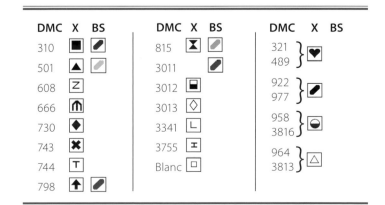

DMC	X	BS		DMC	X	BS		DMC	X	BS
310	■	◢		815	⊠	◢		321		
501	▲	◢		3011		◢		489	♥	
608	Z			3012	▣			922		
666	⋔			3013	◇			977	◢	
730	◆			3341	L			958		
743	✖			3755	I			3816	⬒	
744	T			Blanc	▢			964		
798	↑	◢						3813	△	

Oriental Kimono

Design Information

Design stitched on 14-count ivory Aida using 3 strands for Cross Stitch, 1 strand for Straight Stitch, 1 strand for Backstitch, and 1 strand for French Knots.

Blends

1 strand 340 and 2 strands 553
1 strand 350 and 2 strands 351
2 strands 436 and 2 strands **5282
1 strand 563 and 2 strands 597
2 strands 741 and 2 strands *002 HL
2 strands 743 and 2 strands *002 HL
1 strand 931 and 2 strands 793
1 strand 3363 and 2 strands 912
* Kreinik Blending Filament
** DMC Light Effects

Stitch Count

158w X 170h in stitches

Design Size

11½w X 12⅜h inches on 14-count fabric

Add 4–6 inches to each measurement for cut fabric size.

DMC	X	BS	Str	FK	DMC	X	BS	Str	FK
211	◇				3824	H			
310	■	◢	◢	●	Blanc	□			
319	◆				340 / 553	⬆			
350	L				350 / 351	◢			
352	⊕				436 / 5282	★			
368	✠				563 / 597	Z			
369	I				741 / 002	◮			
519	4				743 / 002	⋒			
597	◣				931 / 793	⊡			
666	⋔				3363 / 912	⊖			
741	✚								
743	△								
745	T								
794	✖								
919	♥	◢							
3345	✖	◢							
3811	V								

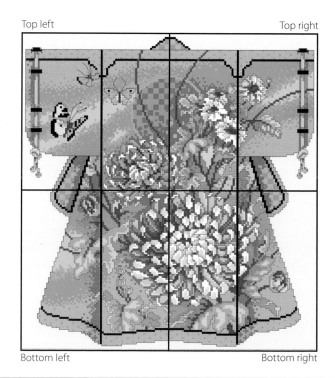

Top left   Top right

Bottom left   Bottom right

Greyed stitches indicate last row from previous section of design.

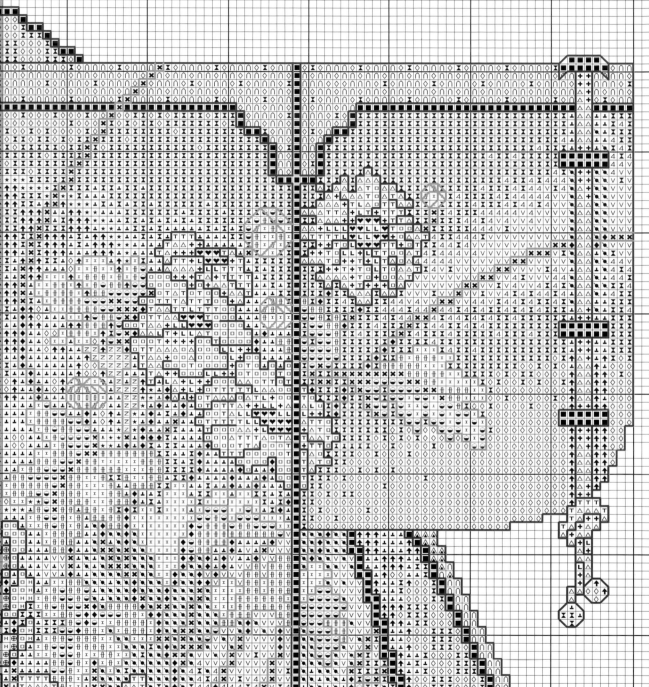

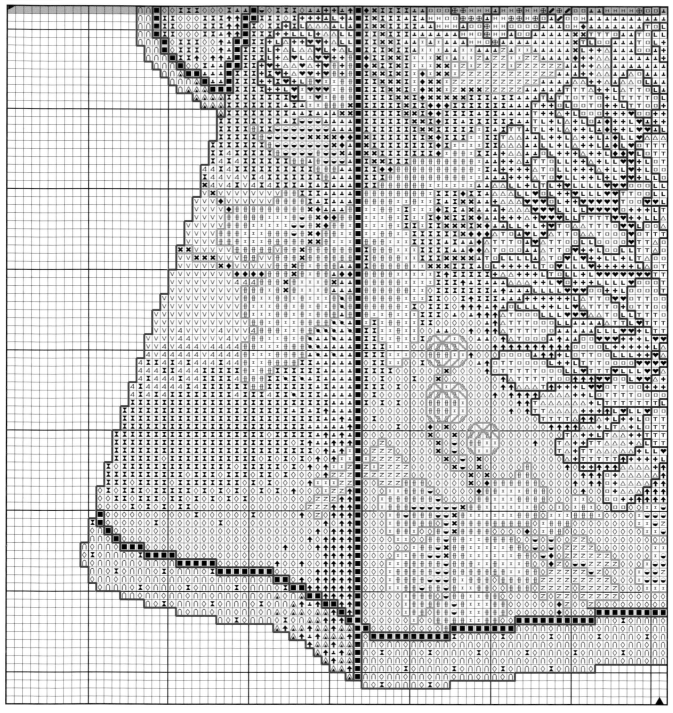

Greyed stitches indicate last row from previous section of design.

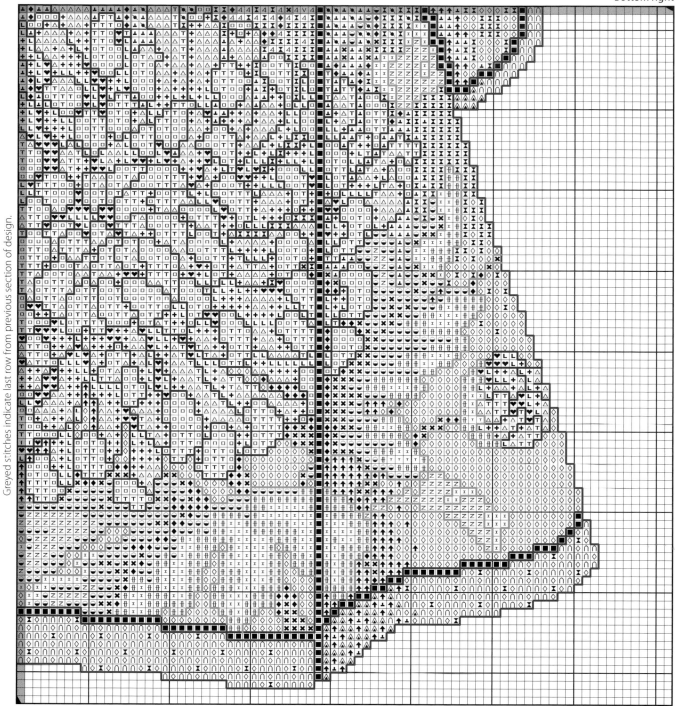

Country
Nasturtium

Design Information
Design stitched on 28-count antique white Monaco over two threads using 3 strands for Cross Stitch and 1 strand for Backstitch.

Blends
1 strand 721 and 2 strands 741
1 strand Blanc and 2 strands 504

Stitch Count
173w X 124h in stitches

Design Size
12⅝w X 9⅛h inches on 28-count antique white fabric stitched over two threads

Add 4–6 inches to each measurement for cut fabric size.

DMC	X	BS	DMC	X	BS
347	✖	◤	890	◆	◤
469	⊠	◤	976	▣	
471	◤		3347	⊙	
501	⬆		3348	2	
504	T		3813	◨	
608	4		3816	⋔	
676	△		3826	⊥	◹
742	◭		Blanc	▢	◹
744	H		721 } ●		
745	⊤		741		
772	L		Blanc } +		
801	■		504		
814	♥	◤			

Top left · Top right

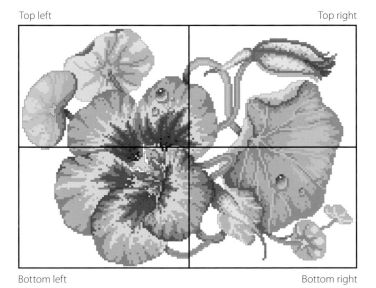

Bottom left · Bottom right

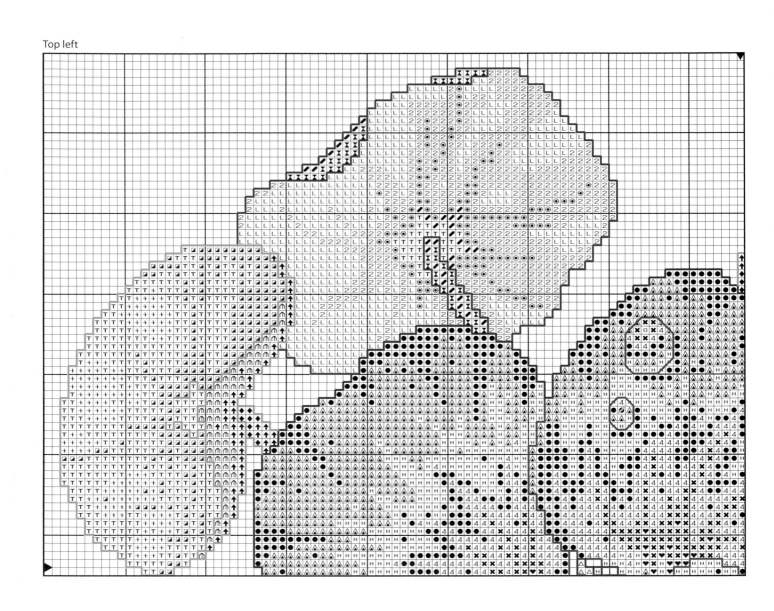

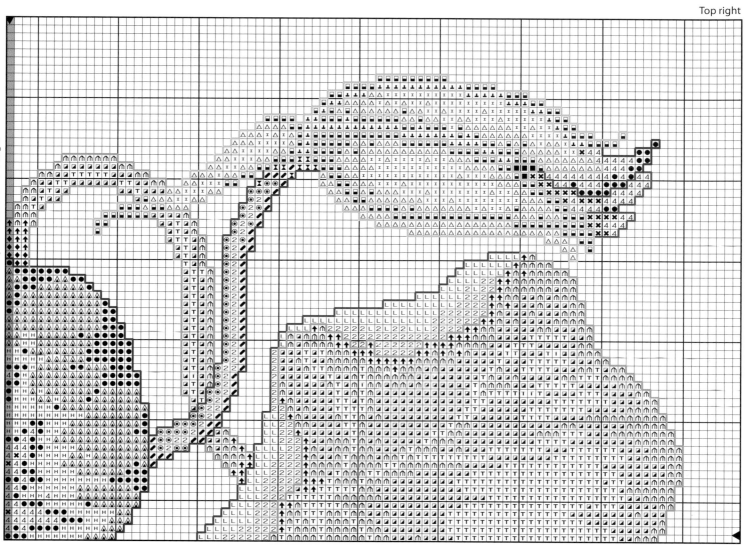

Greyed stitches indicate last row from previous section of design.

Bottom left

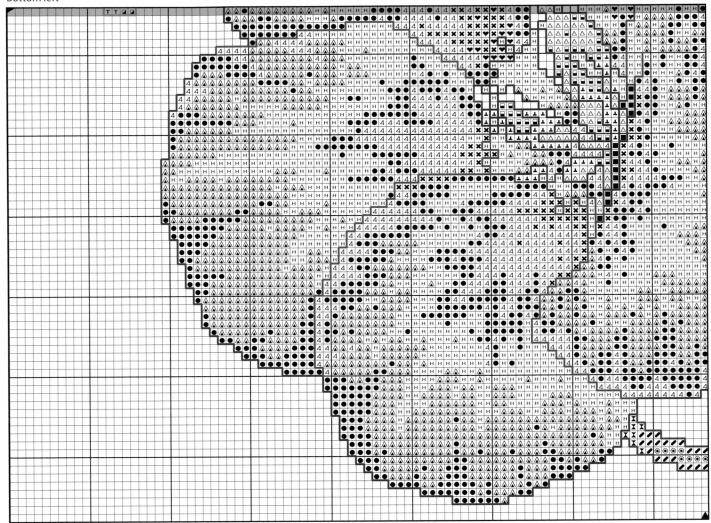

Greyed stitches indicate last row from previous section of design.

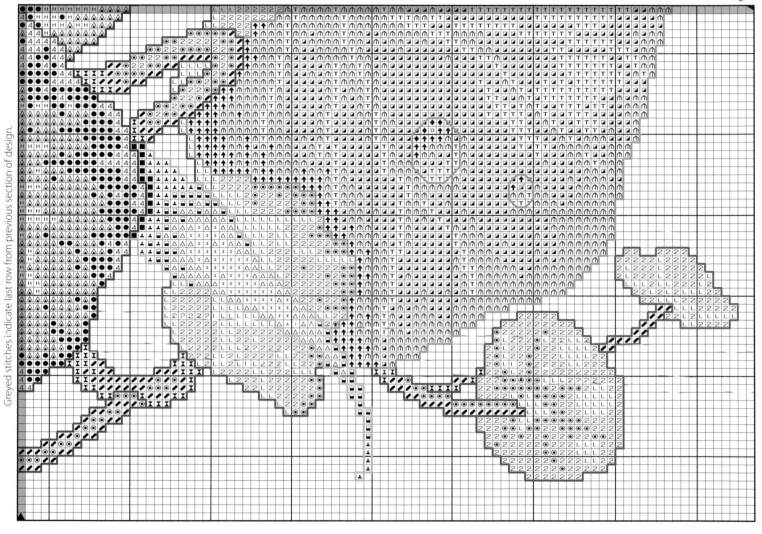

Sandy Orton

Sandy has had a lifelong interest in all types of traditional handiwork, crafts and gardening, often bestowing the appreciative studio staff with the fruits of her bountiful garden. Her background and artistic experience have been a great match for Kooler Design Studio, where she started working in 1993. Sandy's keen interest in textiles of all kinds and her love of intricate embroidery are reflected in her work which often uses elaborate stitches and techniques from all periods of history. Her designs are sought out by expert stitchers, and her perfectly detailed samplers are easily recognized by the discerning eye and coveted by collectors.

Chapter 3

Bless Our
Family

Design Information

Design stitched on 14-count white Aida using 3 strands for Full and ¼ Cross Stitch, 1 & 2 strands for Backstitch, and 1 strand for French Knots.

Stitch Count

170w X 224h in stitches

Design Size

12⅜w X 16¼h inches on 14-count fabric

Add 4–6 inches to each measurement for cut fabric size.

DMC	X	¼	BS	FK	DMC	X	¼	BS	FK
333	+	+	/	●	814	↑			
340	7	7			898	✖	✖		●
347	⊙				920	♥			
350	C				945	L	L		
434	↓	↓	/		986	♠	♠		
453	◇	◇	/		987	⊞	⊞	/	
471	✚	+			989	◑	◑		
501	▣	▣	/		3371	■	■	/	
502	◢	◢			3687	⊥	⊥		
503	e	e			3688	V	V		
535	◆	◆		●	3689	♡	♡		
646	2	2			3746	▲	▲		
647	目	目		●	3803	✕	✕	/	●
676	★	★			3828	◗	◗		
677	H				3829*	◈	◈	/	
680	4	4			3838	⋔	⋔	/	
721	∩	∩			3839	⌐	⌐		●
722	◣				3840	◌	◌		
729	//	//			Blanc	□	□		
746	⊥								

*Use 2 strands for Backstitch.

Top left   Top right

Bottom left   Bottom right

BLESS OUR FAMILY

A FAMILY'S ROOTS RUN DEEP AND TRUE

A FAMILY IS A CIRCLE OF CARING AND SHARING

25th ANNIVERSARY

Family is LOVE

1950 51

HARRIET 11·12·84

JONATHAN 9·26·88

The Apple does not Fall far from the Tree

ALEXANDRA HAMPTON 9·25·55

MICHAEL ANDERSON 10·30·53

MARRIED APRIL 30, 1980

Blessed is the family whose trust is in the LORD

1234567890
ABCDEFGHIJKL
MNOPQRSTUVW
XYZ abcdefghi
jklmnopqrstuvwxyz

GOD BLESS US EVERYONE

A FAMILY'S ROOTS

25th

ANNIVERSARY

Personalization line (Do not stitch.)

RUN DEEP AND TRUE

Personalization line (Do not stitch.)

Greyed stitches indicate last row from previous section of design.

My Old-fashioned
Paper Doll

Design Information

Design stitched on 14-count white Aida using 3 strands for Full and ¼ Cross Stitch 1 & 2 strands for Backstitch, and 1 strand for French Knots.

Blends

1 strand 223 and 2 strands 335
1 strand 3824 and 2 strands 3326

Stitch Count

168w X 154h in stitches

Design Size

12¼w X 11¼h inches on 14-count fabric

Add 4–6 inches to each measurement for cut fabric size.

DMC	X	¼	BS	FK	DMC	X	¼	BS	FK
209					798				●
211					844				●
309				●	899				
310				●	912				
368					945				
369					954				
407					3325				
433				●	3326				
502					3826				
647					3827				
648					Blanc				●
676					223 }				
744				●	335				
746					3824 }				
758					3326				
760					E5282*				
794									

*Use 2 strands DMC Light Effects for Backstitch.

Top left   Top right

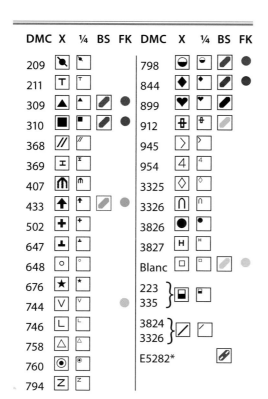

Bottom left   Bottom right

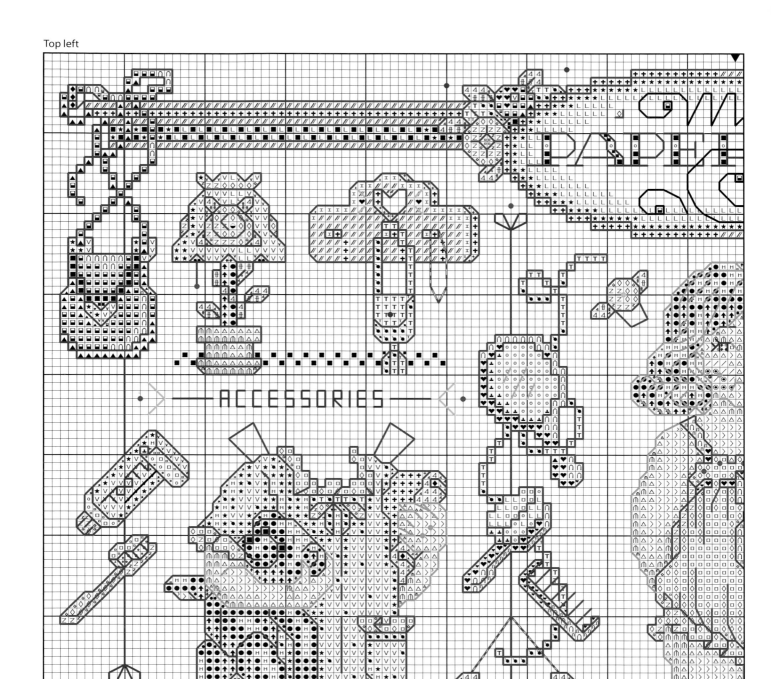

TEA PARTY
DRESS

Greyed stitches indicate last row from previous section of design.

Bottom left

SNUGGLY · PAJAMAS

SET SAIL
MIDDY

Greyed stitches indicate last row from previous section of design.

RY
ZETH

⎯⎯⎯⎯ Personalization line (Do not stitch.)

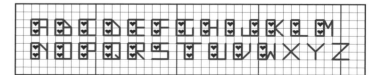

Nature's Wisdom
Sampler

Design Information

Design stitched on 14-count white Aida using 3 strands for Cross Stitch and 1 strand for Backstitch.

Stitch Count

149w X 191h in stitches

Design Size

10⅞w X 13⅞h inches on 14-count fabric

Add 4–6 inches to each measurement for cut fabric size.

DMC	X	BS	DMC	X	BS
208	▣		772	C	
209	⊞		799	◣	
211	H		818	V	
320	⊥		828	T	
351	◪		838	■	▱
367	⬆		921	◆	
433	⊠		962	e	
435	L		989	⊠	
470	♠		3041	✚	▱
471	Z		3042	●	
501	▲		3348	❭	
502	◢		3350	✖	
503	a		3354	✚	
519	˥		3731	◒	
554	4		3743	ⶫ	
727	⊘		3746	//	
729	⋔		3803	♥	
741	★		3823	ɾu	
742	⊠		Blanc	▢	
743	◇				

Top left · Top right

Bottom left · Bottom right

THE BEAUTY OF EACH · BLOSSOM · SPEAKS SILENTLY OF LOVE

The Beauty of Each
• Blossom •
Speaks Silently
Of Love

Top right

Ty OF EACH
SSOM

Greyed stitches indicate last row from previous section of design.

Greyed stitches indicate last row from previous section of design.

To Everything
There Is a Season

Design Information

Design stitched on 14-count oatmeal Fiddler's Aida using 3 strands for Full and ¼ Cross Stitch, 1 strand for Backstitch, and 1 strand for French Knots.

Blends

1 strand 340 and 2 strands 3746
1 strand 351 and 2 strands 350
1 strand 436 and 2 strands 435
1 strand 501 and 2 strands 500
1 strand 760 and 2 strands 223
1 strand 3721 and 2 strands 3722

Stitch Count

168w X 224h in stitches

Design Size

12½w X 16⅜h inches on 14-count fabric

Add 4–6 inches to each measurement for cut fabric size.

DMC	X	¼	BS	FK	DMC	X	¼	BS	FK
208	⊕	⊕			3011	▣	▣		
209	△				3012	◮	◮		
301	▣		◢		3371	■	▪		
333	⋔	⋔	◢		3802	♥			
341	⊥	⊥		●	3831	✛	✛		●
350	2			●	3853	⊠			
434	◣				3854	‡			
435	∥				3862	✖	✖		
471	4	4			3864	∩	∩		
500			◢		340 / 3746	❯	❯		
502	◉	◉			351 / 350	7			
648	∨	∨			436 / 435	e			
676	★	★			501 / 500	◆	◆		
677	H	H			760 / 223	C			
729	◇	◇			3721 / 3722	⊥			
734	⊞	⊞							
746	L	L							
898	⬆	⬆	◢	●					
918	✚								
988	Z	z							

Top left   Top right

·AUTUMN·
Oak & Acorn
Squirrel
Pheasant
Maple Leaf
ABCDEFGHIJK
LMNOPQRSTU
VWXYZabcdef
ghijklmnoPqrst
uvwxyz1234567
Apple tree
Pear tree
·To Everything·
·there is a Season·

Bottom left   Bottom right

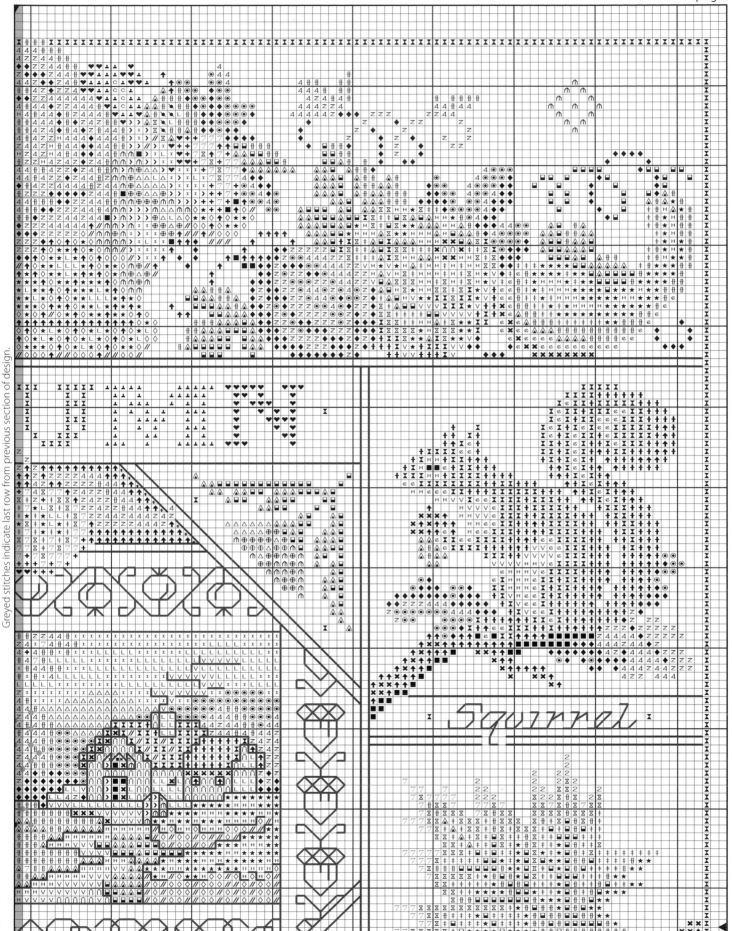

Pheasant

Apple tree

Everything

Bottom right

Maple Leaf
Pear tree
there is a eason

Greyed stitches indicate last row from previous section of design.

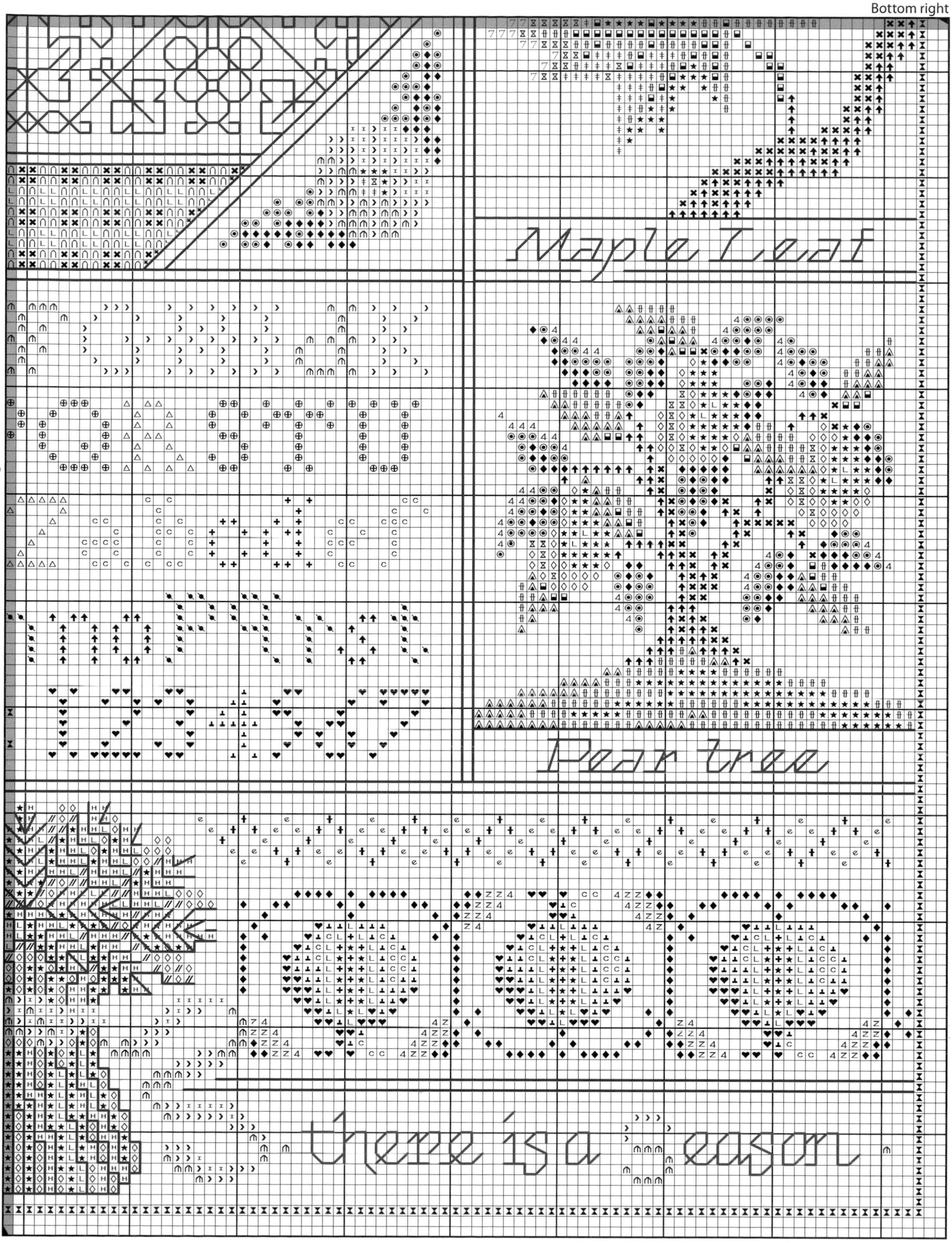

The Lord Is My
Shepherd

Design Information

Design stitched on 14-count white Aida using 3 strands for Full and ¼ Cross Stitch, 1 strand for ½ Cross Stitch, 1 & 2 strands for Backstitch, and 1 strand for French Knots.

Blends

1 strand 436 and 2 strands 435
1 strand 794 and 2 strands 793
1 strand 519 and 2 strands 827
1 strand 793 and 2 strands 3042
1 strand 3041 and 2 strands 3042
1 strand 3727 and 2 strands 794

Stitch Count

154w X 224h in stitches

Design Size

11¼w X 16¼h inches on 14-count fabric

Add 4–6 inches to each measurement for cut fabric size.

DMC	X	¼	½	BS	FK
322	▲	▲		◹	●
353	❯				
434	◣	◣			
435	◈	◈			
436	✚	✚			
437	O	º			
472	╱	╱			
501	⬕	⬕			
502	♠	♠			
612	⬓	⬓			
640	⬆	⬆			
677	★	★			
745	◇	◇			
746	Ⅱ	Ⅱ			
760	♥	♥			
792	✖	✖		◹	●
793	⊖	⊖			
794	▣	▪			
828	∩				
838	■	■		◹	
838*				◹	
3011	◆	◆		◹	
3012	⬇	⬇			

*Use 2 strands.

DMC	X	¼	½	BS	FK
3041	✚	✚			
3042	T	T	◹		
3046	C	C			
3363	⊥	⊥			
3364	⊘	⊘			
3727	△				
3740	♣	♣			
3743	H	H			
3756	L				
3781	●	•		◹	
3782	V	V			
3790	⊞	⊞			
436 / 435	⋔	⋔			
794 / 793	∥	∥			
519 / 827	4	4			
793 / 3042	⬇				
3041 / 3042	2	2			
3727 / 794	Z				

Top left · Top right · Bottom left · Bottom right

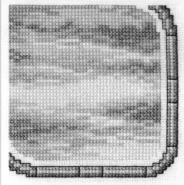
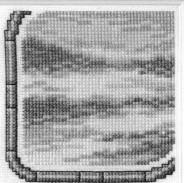

The Lord is My
Shepherd,
I shall not want; he
makes me lie down
in green pastures.
He leads me beside

the still waters,
he restores my soul.
He leads me in the
paths of righteousness
for his name's sake.

The
23RD
PSALM

Even though I walk
through the valley of
the shadow of death,
I fear no evil; for
thou art with me; thy

Rod and thy staff
they comfort me
Thou preparest a
table before
me in the presence
of my enemies; thou
anointest my head
* with oil *
my cup overflows.
Surely * goodness
and mercy shall
follow me all the days
of my life; + I shall
dwell in the house of
the LORD forever
*

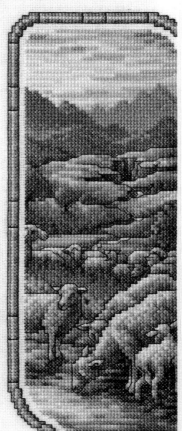

Top right

Greyed stitches indicate last row from previous section of design.

Bottom right

Greyed stitches indicate last row from previous section of design.

Cutting line for Evenweave

Bookmark:
Hummingbirds

Design Information

Design stitched on ivory 28-count Monaco Evenweave over 2 threads using 3 strands for Cross Stitch, 1 strand for Straight Stitch, 1 & 2 strands for Backstitch, and 1 strand for French Knots.

Backing

Kunin Felt #8H3 Walnut Brown 3¼" X 9"

Stitch Count

34w X 106h in stitches

Design Size

2⅝w X 7¾h inches on 28-count Evenweave over 2 threads
Add 4–6 inches to each measurement for cut fabric size.

Finishing

See page 7 for finishing instructions.

DMC	X	BS	Str	FK
472	◇			
603	⊥			
605	L			
646	◩	▱		
648	4		▱	
838	■	▱		●
838*		▱		
844	◆			
3072	⌐			
3362		▱		
3363	✚			
3364	⊙			
3803	♥	▱		
3805	✖			
3862	⬆			
3863	H			
Blanc*	☐	▱		●

* Use 2 strands for Backstitch.

Cutting line for Aida

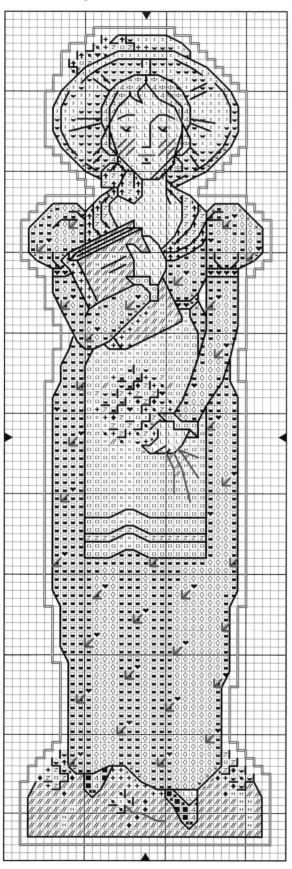

Bookmark:

A Lady and Her Book

Design Information
Design stitched on 14-count ivory Aida using 3 strands for Cross Stitch, 1 and 2 strands for Backstitch, and 1 strand for French Knots.

Backing
Kunin Felt #8H3 Walnut Brown 3¼" X 9"

Stitch Count
31w X 102h in stitches

Design Size
2½w X 7½h inches on 14-count fabric
Add 4–6 inches to each measurement for cut fabric size.

Finishing
See page 7 for finishing instructions.

DMC	X	¼	BS
676	⊖	⊖	
677	I	I	
772	H		
932	⬆	⬆	
948	L	L	
962	◣		
963	◇	◇	
3072	○		
3348	∥	∥	
3363*	◆	◆	◢
3364	✚	✚	
3687*	♥	♥	◢
3716*	◪	◪	◢
3752	Z	Z	
3862	■	■	◢
3862*			◢
3863	4	4	
3864	⊞		
Blanc	☐	☐	

* Use 2 strands for Backstitch.

Bookmark:
Mr. Atomic

Design Information

Design stitched on 14-count Lemon Twist Aida using 3 strands for Full and ¼ Cross Stitch, 1 & 2 strands for Backstitch, and 1 strand for French Knots.

Backing

Kunin Felt #937 Black 3¼" X 9"

Stitch Count

35w X 101h in stitches

Design Size

2¾w X 7½h inches on 14-count fabric

Add 4–6 inches to each measurement for cut fabric size.

Finishing

See page 7 for finishing instructions.

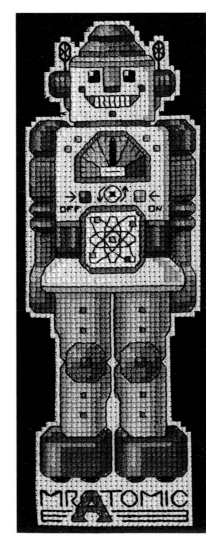

DMC	X	¼	BS
157			
310			
310*			
349			
350			
472			
700			
702			
704			
741			
742			
797			
798			
799			
3078			
Blanc			

* Use 2 strands for Backstitch.

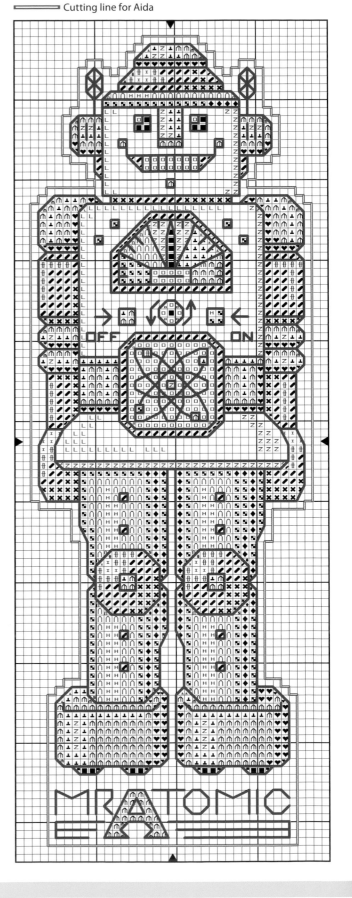

Cutting line for Aida

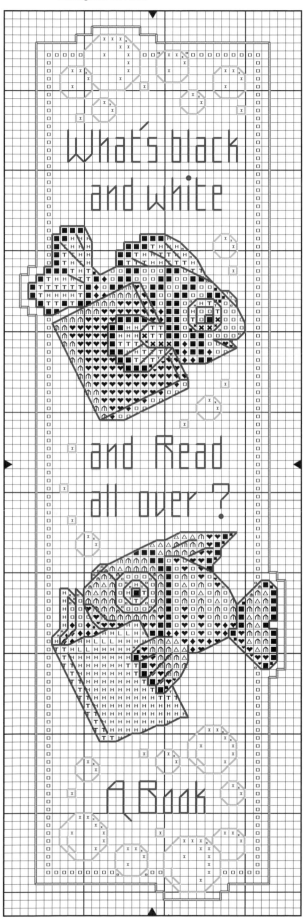

Bookmark:
Fish School

Design Information

Design stitched on 14-count Polar Ice Aida using 3 strands for Cross Stitch, 1 & 2 strands for Backstitch, and 1 strand for French Knots.

Backing

Kunin Felt #937 Black 3¼" X 9"

Stitch Count

33w X 109h in stitches

Design Size

2⅝w X 8h inches on 14-count fabric

Add 4–6 inches to each measurement for cut fabric size.

Finishing

See page 7 for finishing instructions.

DMC	X	BS	FK
310	■	╱	●
310*		╱	
350	♥		
351	⋔		
352	△		
415	◆		
726	□		
741	✖		
742	T		
747	I		
3078	L		
3843		╱	
Blanc	□		

* Use 2 strands for Backstitch.

Bookmark:
Monkey See, Monkey Do

Design Information
Design stitched on 14-count Lemon Twist Aida using 3 strands for Cross Stitch, 1 & 2 strands for Backstitch, and 1 strand for French Knots.

Backing
Kunin Felt #8H3 Walnut Brown 3¼" X 9"

Blend
1 strand 839 and 2 strands 543

Stitch Count
35w X 105h in stitches

Design Size
2¾w X 7¾h inches on 14-count fabric

Add 4–6 inches to each measurement for cut fabric size.

Finishing
See page 7 for finishing instructions.

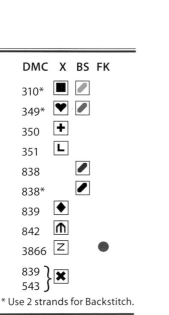

DMC	X	BS	FK
310*	■	╱	
349*	♥	╱	
350	✚		
351	L		
838		╱	
838*		╱	
839	◆		
842	⋔		
3866	Z		●
839 }	✖		
543 }			

* Use 2 strands for Backstitch.

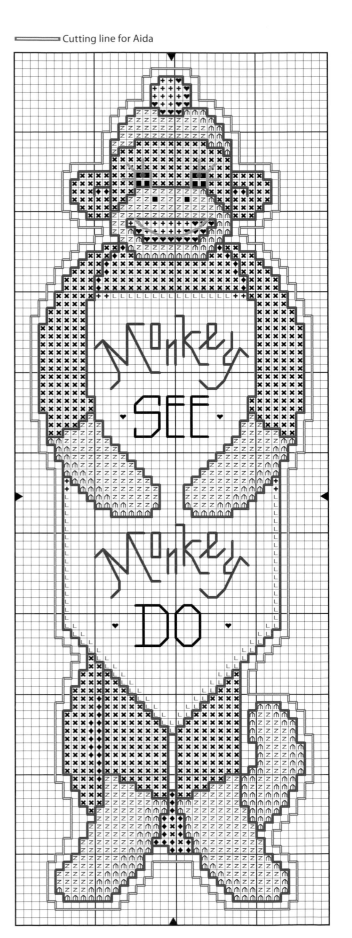

Cutting line for Aida

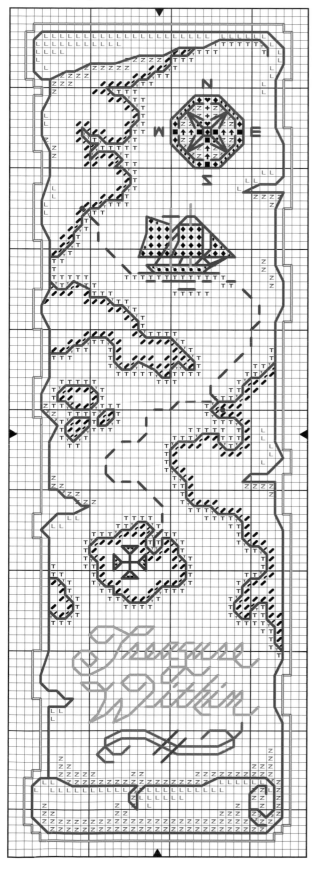

Bookmark: Treasure Within

Design Information

Design stitched on 14-count beige Aida using 2 & 3 strands for Cross Stitch, 1 & 2 strands for Backstitch, and 1 strand for French Knots.

Backing

Kunin Felt #8H3 Walnut Brown 3¼" x 9"

Stitch Count

33w X 102h in stitches

Design Size

2⅝w X 7½h inches on 14-count fabric

Add 4–6 inches to each measurement for cut fabric size.

Finishing

See page 7 for finishing instructions.

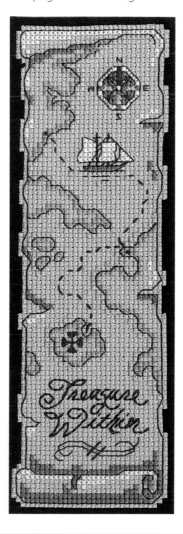

DMC	X	BS	FK
349*	♥	◢	●
349		◢	
350	✚		
598	⬆		
598**	T		
712	◆		
712**	L		
826	■		
839*		◢	
839		◢	
989**	◢		
3862	◣		
3863	Z		

* Use 2 strands for Backstitch.
**Use 2 strands for Cross Stitch.

Give Us Lord,
a Bit o' Sun

Design Information
Design stitched on 14-count white Aida using 3 strands for Full, ½, and ¼ Cross Stitch, 1 & 2 strands for Backstitch, and 1 strand for French Knots.

Stitch Count
169w X 140h in stitches

Design Size
12¼w X 10¼h inches on 14-count fabric

Add 4–6 inches to each measurement for cut fabric size.

Top left · Top right · Bottom left · Bottom right

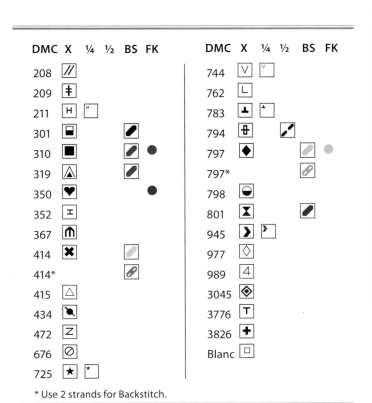

DMC	X	¼	½	BS	FK		DMC	X	¼	½	BS	FK
208	//						744	V	v			
209	‡						762	L				
211	H	H					783	⊥	⊤			
301	▣			╱			794	⊞			╱	
310	■			╱	●		797	◆			╱	●
319	▲			╱			797*				╱	
350	♥				●		798	◓				
352	I						801	✕			╱	
367	⋒						945	❭	❯			
414	✖			╱			977	◇				
414*				╱			989	4				
415	△						3045	◈				
434	◣						3776	T				
472	Z						3826	✚				
676	⊘						Blanc	▢				
725	★	*										

* Use 2 strands for Backstitch.

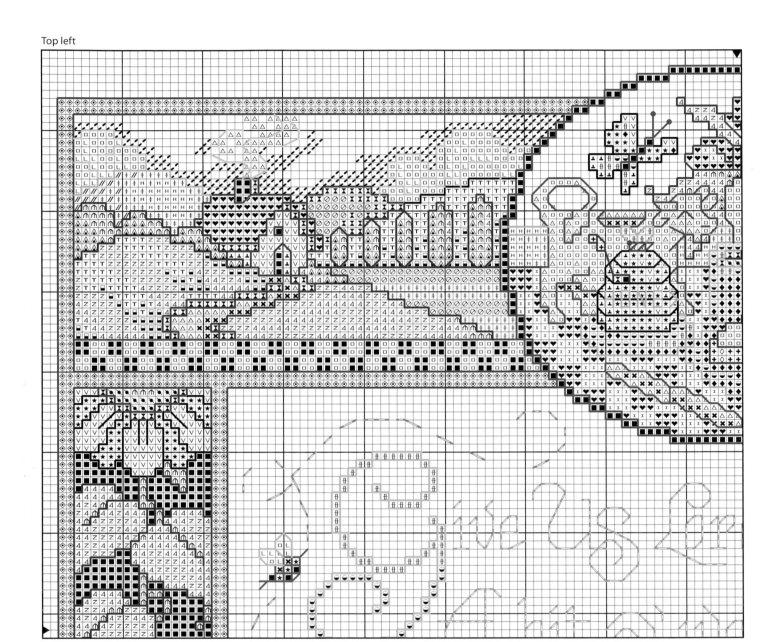

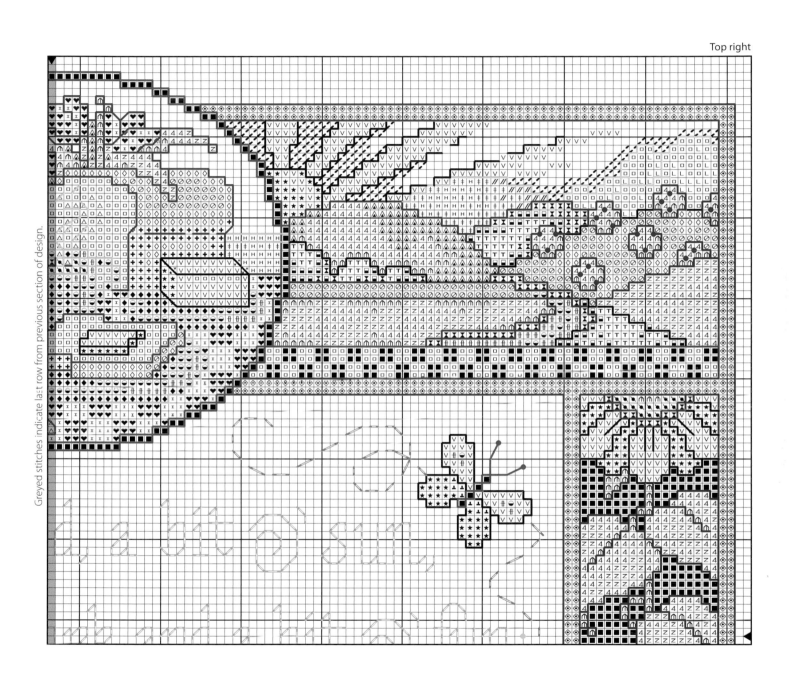

Bottom left

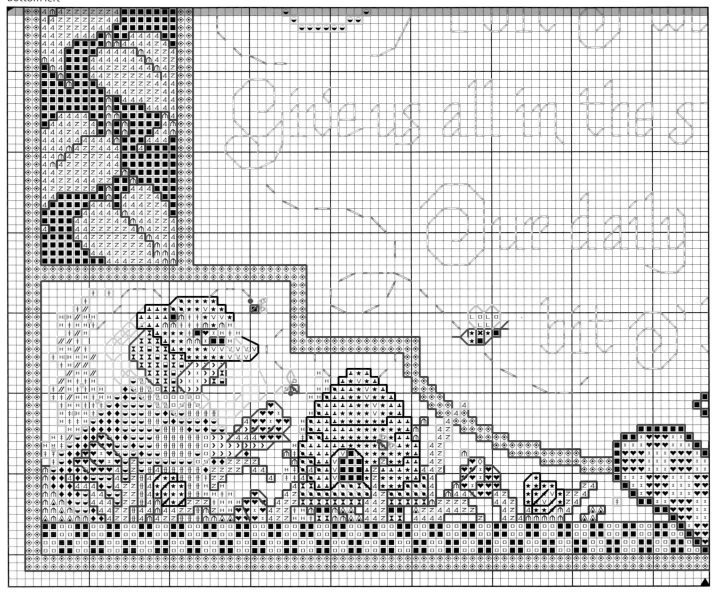

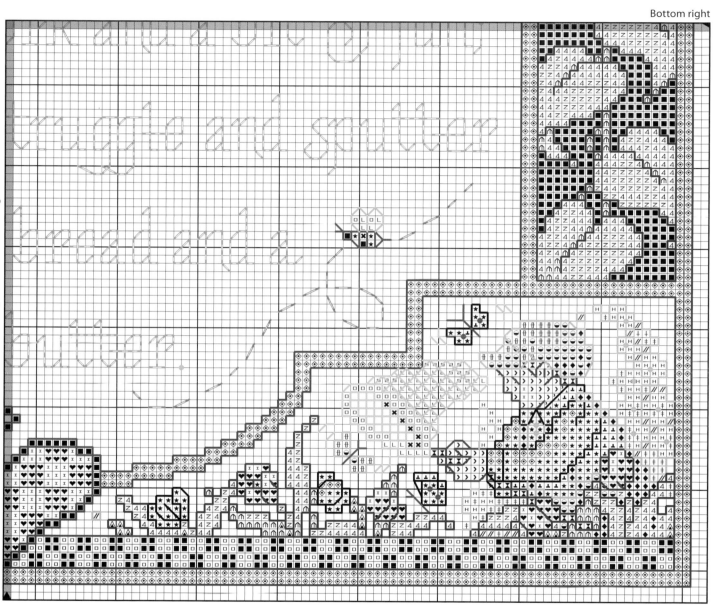

Greyed stitches indicate last row from previous section of design.

Simple Blessings
Sampler

Design Information
Design stitched on 28-count tea-dyed linen over 2 threads using 3 strands for Cross Stitch and 1 strand for Backstitch.

Stitch Count
149w X 191h in stitches

Design Size
10⅞w X 13⅞h inches on 28-count fabric

Add 4–6 inches to each measurement for cut fabric size.

DMC	X	BS
304		✏

Top left   Top right

Bottom left   Bottom right

Top left

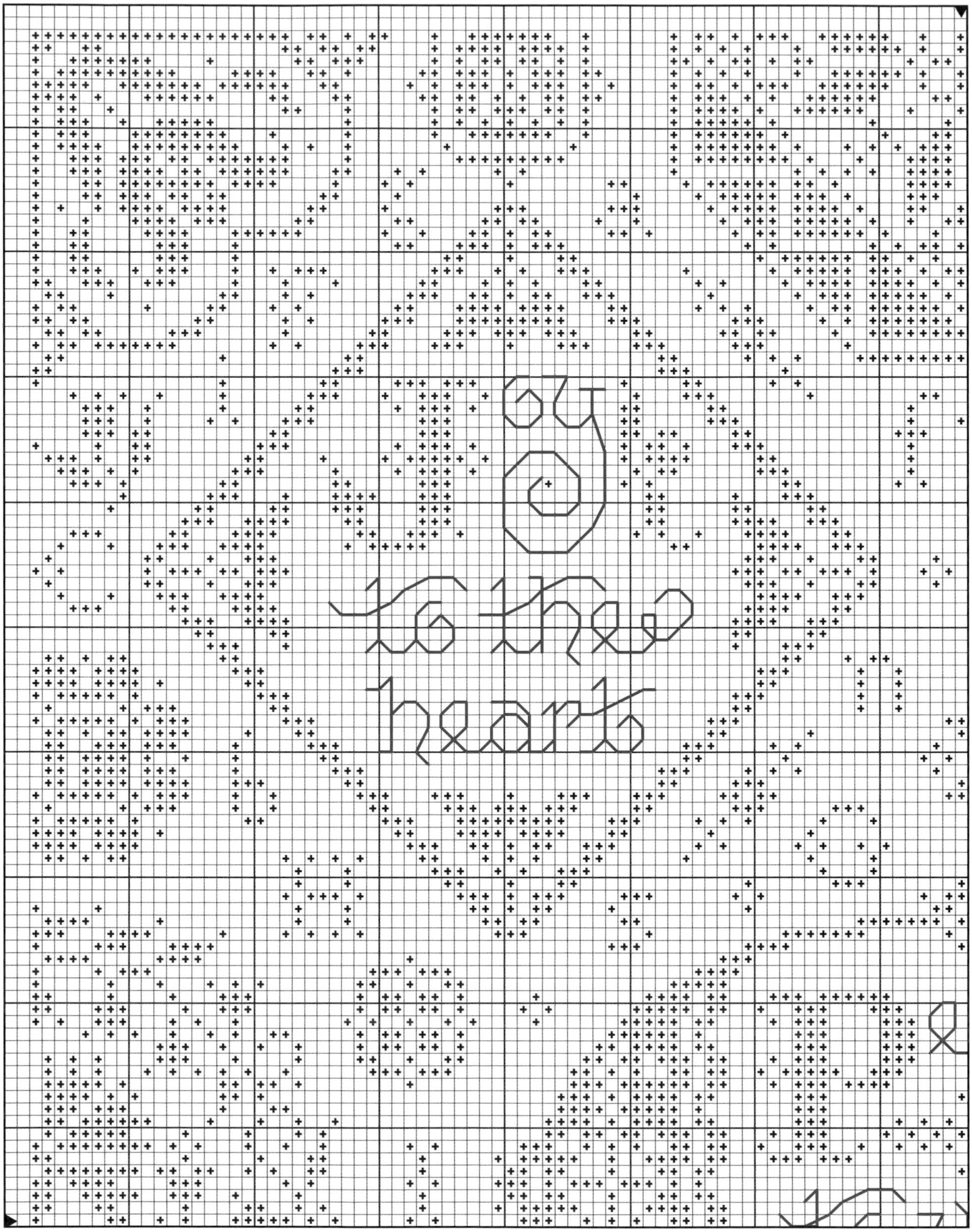

Top right

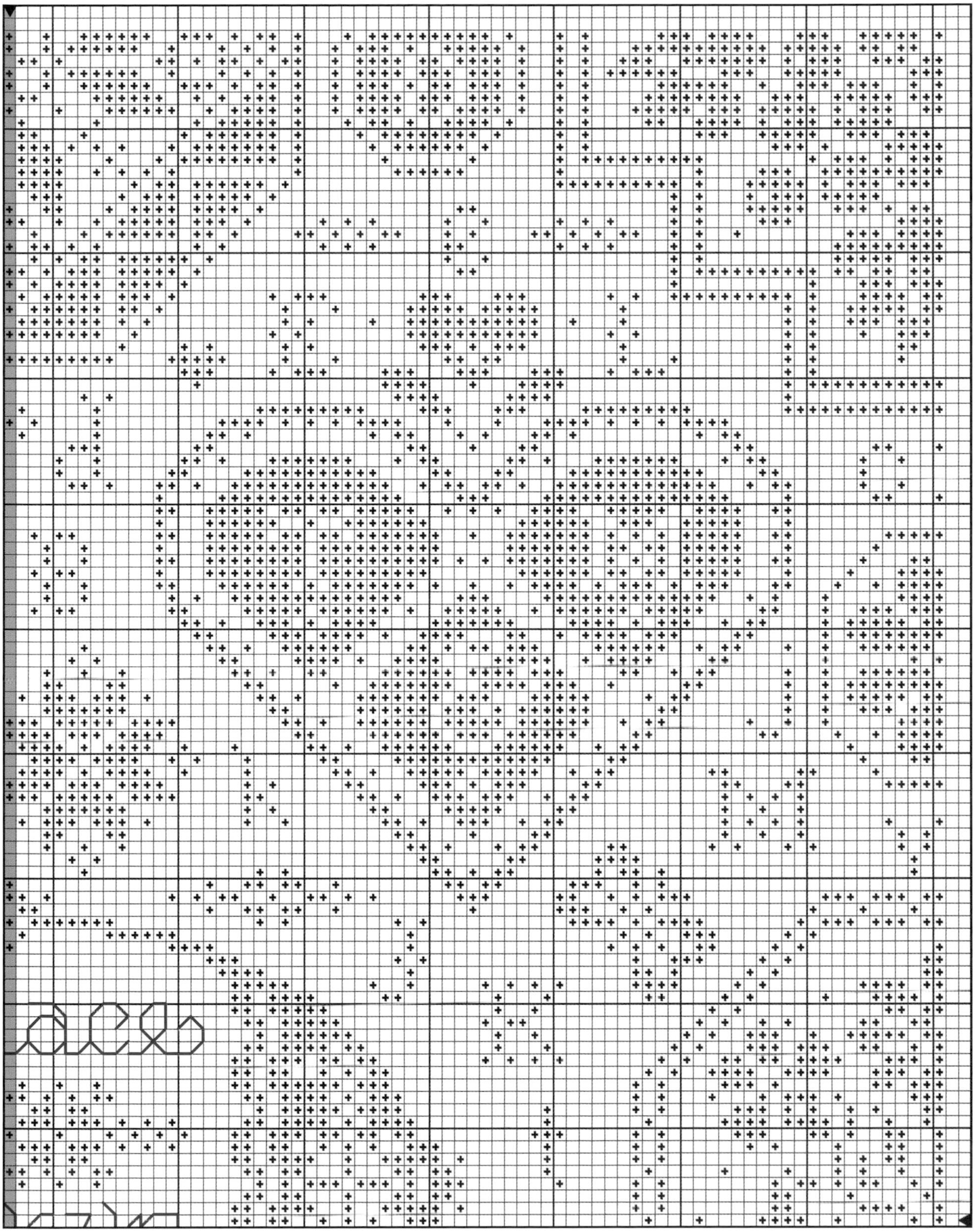

Greyed stitches indicate last row from previous section of design.

Bottom left

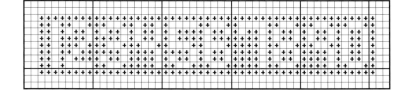

Personalization line (Do not stitch.)

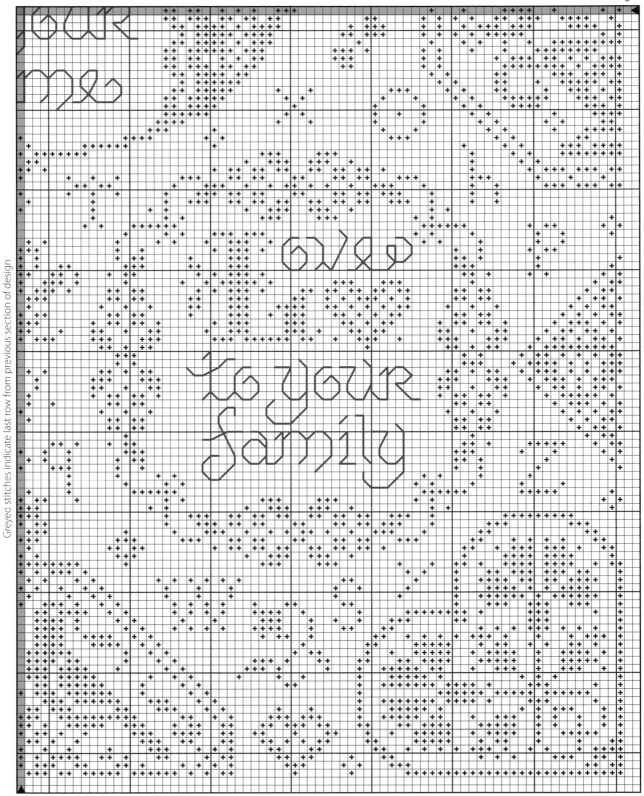

Nancy Rossi

Originally from New England and a graduate of Syracuse University, Nancy found her way to California and has been a key member of Kooler Design Studio since its founding in 1985. Her interest in classic art, illustration, and painting has placed her at the cutting edge of needlework design. Nancy's acute sense of color and composition make her an expert in still life and landscape designs which are diverse and always beautiful. Her understanding of light and how it affects objects gives her work a sense of depth and realism not seen elsewhere in the needlework field. In her spare time Nancy excels in a variety of three dimensional crafts, such as pottery and stained glass; she also loves gardening and renovating her home.

Chapter 4

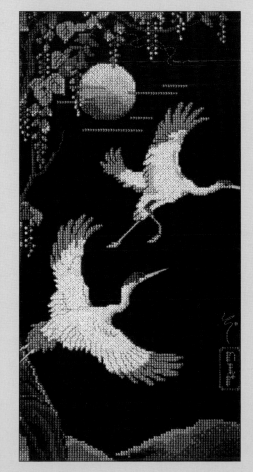

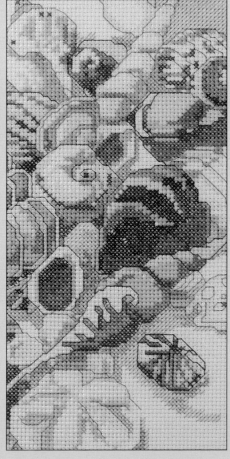

Nancy Rossi

Autumn's Harvest
Wreath

Design Information

Design stitched on 14-count white Aida using 3 strands for Cross Stitch, 1 strand for Backstitch, and 1 strand for Straight Stitch.

Blends

1 strand 740 and 2 strands 742
1 strand 3835 and 2 strands 3746

Stitch Count

194w X 194h in stitches

Design Size

14⅛w X 14⅛h inches on 14-count fabric

Add 4–6 inches to each measurement for cut fabric size.

DMC	X	BS	Str	DMC	X	BS	Str
210	4			977	C		
327	⊥			3012	✚		
351	◈			3013	I		
400	L	▱		3033	❯		
422	∩			3051	⬆	▱	
470	⋔			3721	◩		
471	⊘			3776	◆		
472	Z			3787	◥		
501	⊠	▱		3799	■	▱	▱
504	△			3803	●		
606	⊖			3804	//		
642	‡	▱		3806	V		
666	♥			3816	▣		
721	◉			3835	▱		
726	H			Blanc	▢		
742	★			740 ⎫ 742 ⎬	✚		
841	⬇						
842	⊞			3835 ⎫ 3746 ⎬	✖		
976	↘						

Top left   Top center   Top right

Bottom left   Bottom center   Bottom right

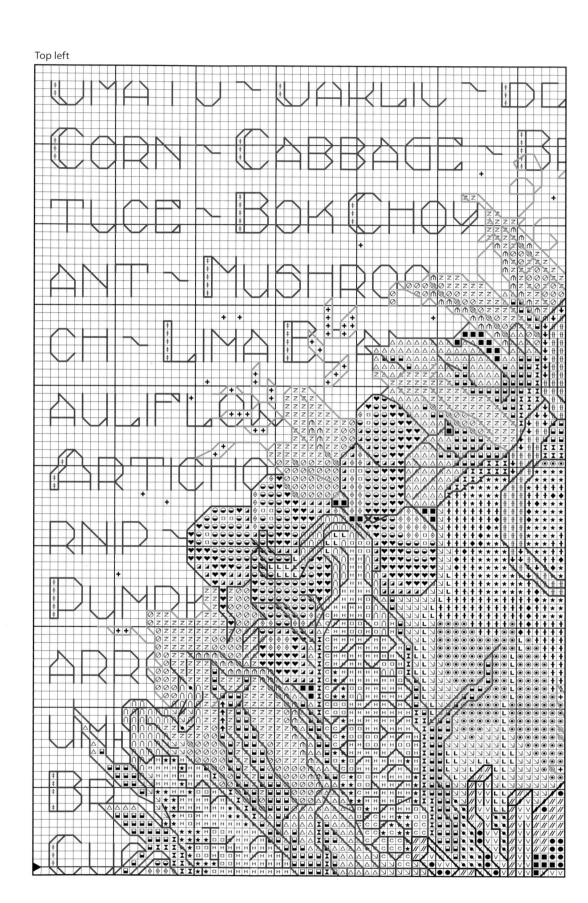

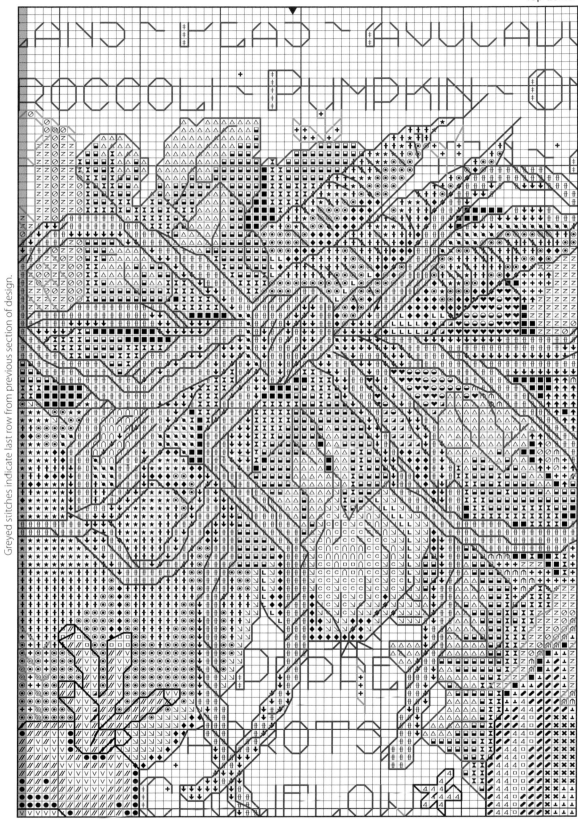

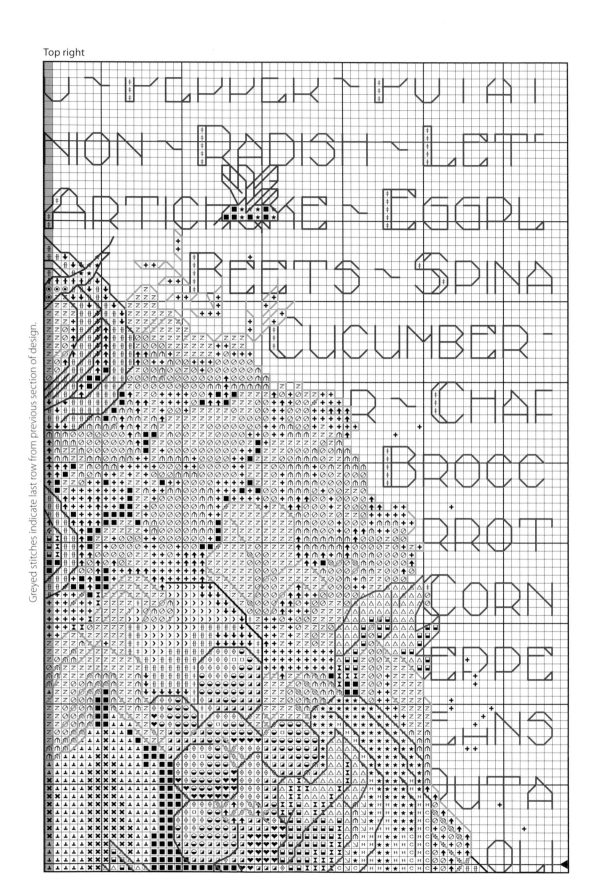

Greyed stitches indicate last row from previous section of design.

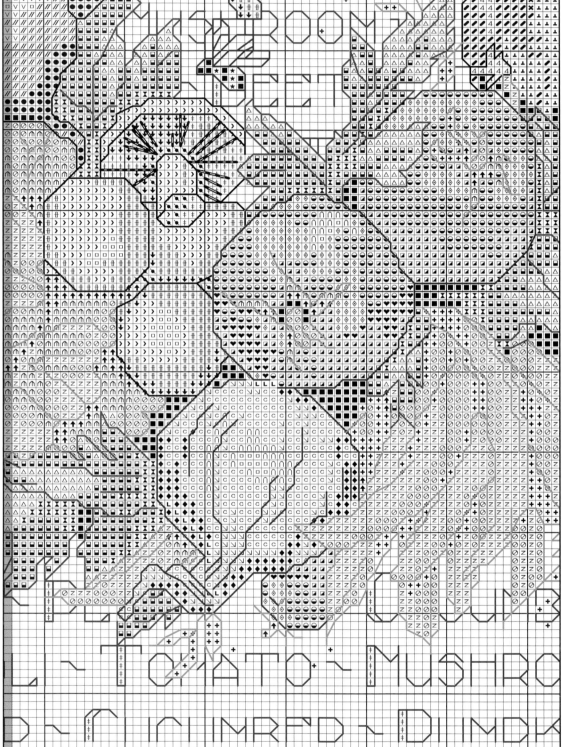

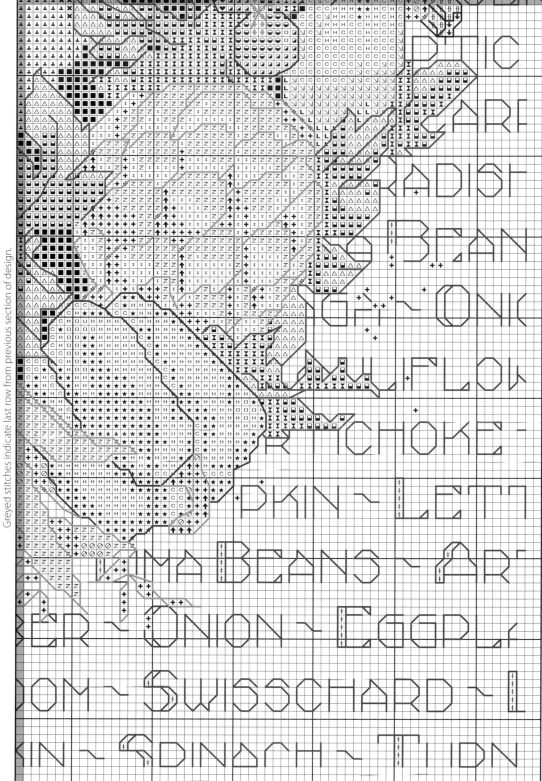

Greyed stitches indicate last row from previous section of design.

Dreaming of Tuscany

Design Information

Design stitched on 14-count beige Aida using 1 & 3 strands for Cross Stitch and 1 strand for Backstitch.

Stitch Count

153w X 194h in stitches

Design Size

11⅛w X 14⅛h inches on 14-count fabric

Add 4–6 inches to each measurement for cut fabric size.

DMC	X	BS		DMC	X	BS
301	←			840	✚	
310	■			841	◈	
367	↑			841*	➤	
402	✚			920	⚓	
402*	◖			932	◉	
433	⊠	▱		976	◪	
433*	⊥			3012	⊟	
436*	℮			3051	●	
470	✖			3052	∕∕	
471	⋒			3078	T	
472	⋈			3752	✕	
523	Z			3776	▱	
613	◇			3778	♥	
677	H			3778*	▤	
726	★			3781	◭	
729	◣			3799	◆	▱
758	⋂			3854	V	
762	△			Blanc	▱	
775	L					

* Use 1 strand for Cross Stitch.

Top left · Top right · Bottom left · Bottom right

Top left

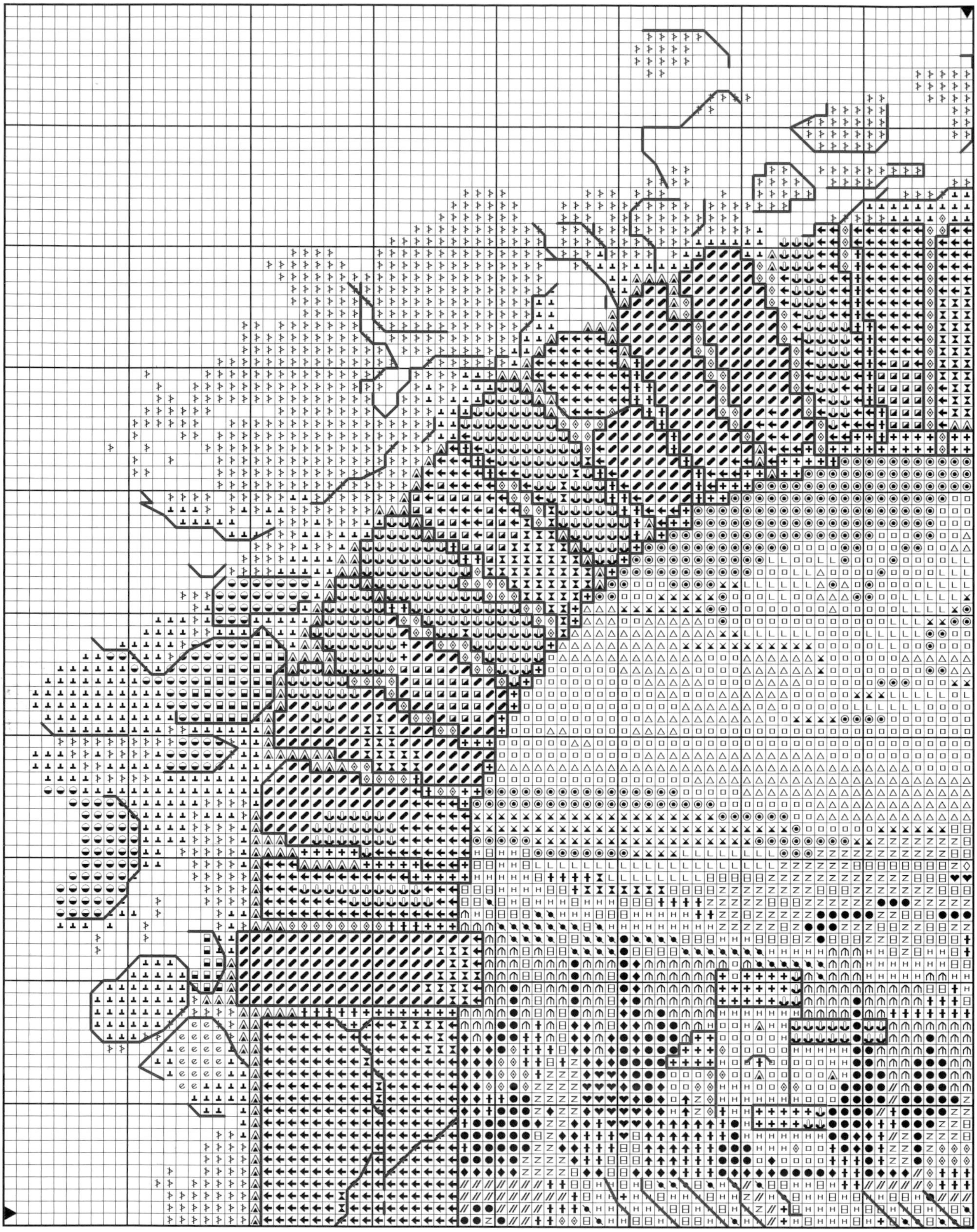

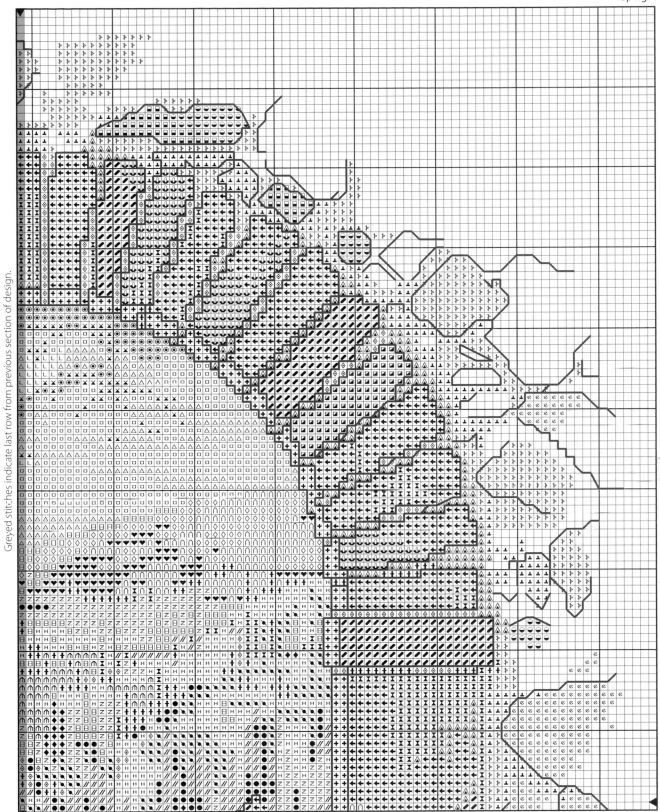

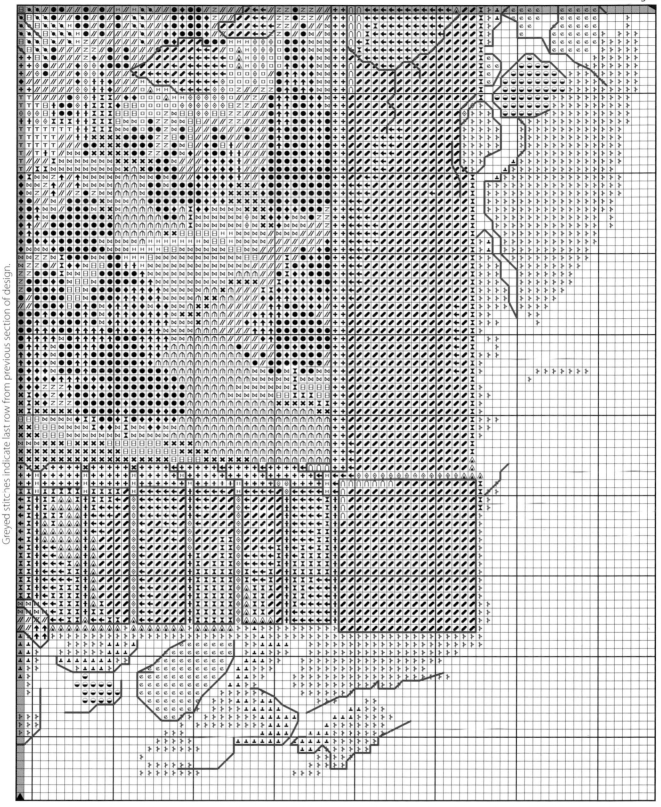

Greyed stitches indicate last row from previous section of design.

Bless Thee
and Keep Thee

Design Information

Design stitched on 14-count beige Aida using 3 strands for Cross Stitch, 1 & 2 strands for Backstitch, and 1 strand for French Knots.

Blends

1 strand 504 and 2 strands 964

1 strand 743 and 2 strands 3854

1 strand 3854 and 1 strand 721

Stitch Count

140w X 224h in stitches

Design Size

10¼w X 16¼h inches on 14-count fabric

Add 4–6 inches to each measurement for cut fabric size.

DMC	X	BS	FK	DMC	X	BS	FK
208	⋔			839	◪	◪	
310	■			841	Z		
327	♥			907	⊥		
333		◪	●	975	⬆		
333*		◪		3013	V		
351	∥			3051	◉	◪	
402	4			3325	L		
434		◪		3363	✕		
452	△			3726	⬇		
453	✕			3776	◢		
472	<			3799	◆	◪	
503	✚			Blanc	▫		
535	▣			504 } 964	⊘		
553	★						
720	◓			743 } 3854	⊞		
738	T						
745	○			3854 } 721	▥		
793	◪						

* Use 2 strands for Backstitch.

Top left · Top right

Bottom left · Bottom right

Greyed stitches indicate last row from previous section of design.

•175•

Birdhouse
Neighborhood

Design Information
Design stitched on 14-count ivory Aida using 3 strands for Cross Stitch, 1 & 2 strands for Straight Stitch, 1 & 2 strands for Backstitch, 1 strand for French Knots, and 2 strands for Couching.

Stitch Count
240w X 110h in stitches

Design Size
17³/₈w X 8¹/₈h inches on 14-count fabric

Add 4–6 inches to each measurement for cut fabric size.

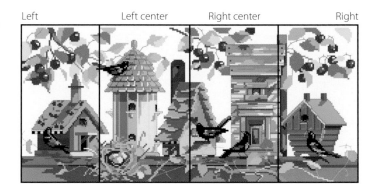

Left   Left center   Right center   Right

DMC	X	BS	Str	FK	Cg	DMC	X	BS	Str	FK	Cg
153	∨					816	✖	⬥			
304	♥					839	▣				
310	■	⬭				841*	◦		⬥		
310*		⬥				930	⬆	⬥			
350	◉					931	◣				
368	∩					959	⊞				
369	H					977	❯				
400	◒					986	⊥				
472	‡				⬭	3363	★	⬥			⬭
553	⧓					3371	◆	⬥	⬥		
704	◇					3756	T				
738*	△		⬥			3776	4				
746	ⱼ					3826	ᛖ				
775	L					3854	Z				
794	⊘					3855	∥				
798	✚					Blanc	▢			●	

* Use 2 strands for Backstitch and Straight Stitch.

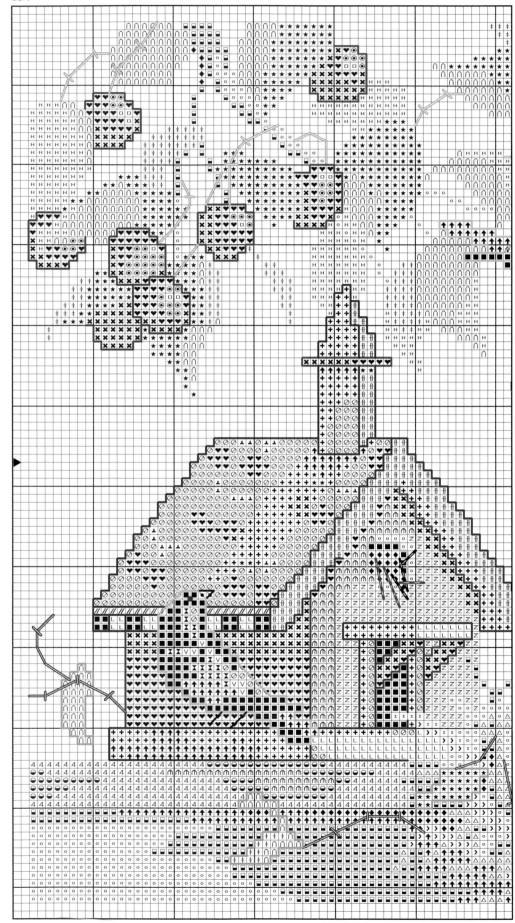

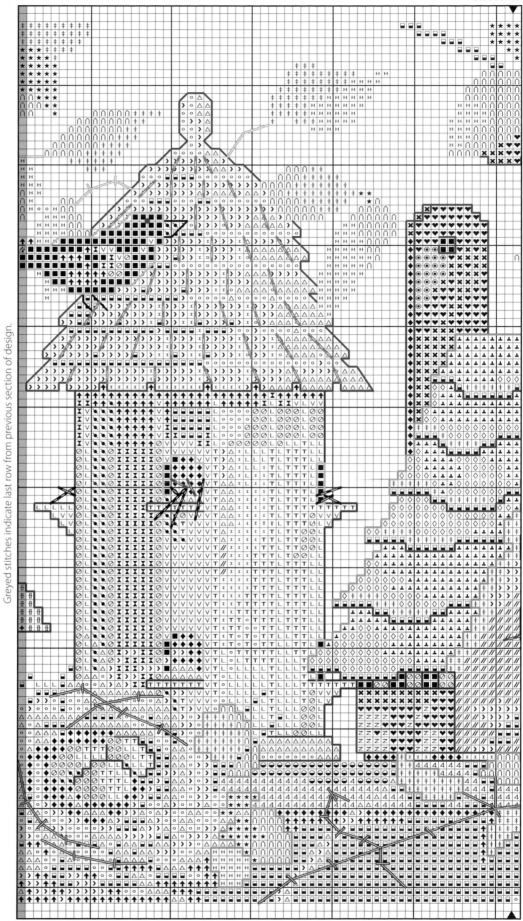

Greyed stitches indicate last row from previous section of design.

Greyed stitches indicate last row from previous section of design.

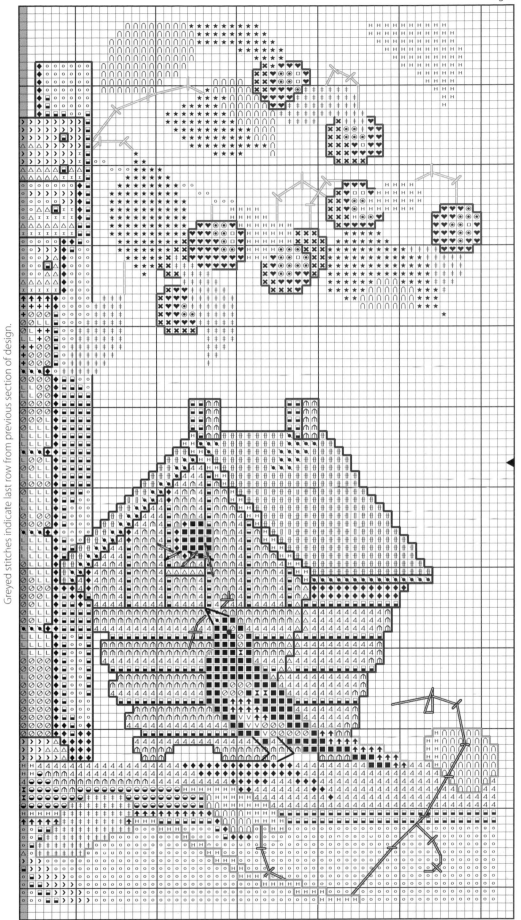

The Woods
Behind My House

Design Information

Design stitched on 14-count Fiddler's Lite Oatmeal Aida using 1 & 3 strands for Cross Stitch, 3 strands for ¼ and ½ Cross Stitch, 1 strand for Backstitch, 1 strand for Straight Stitch, and 1 strand for French Knots.

Blend

1 strand 3790 and 1 strand 451

Stitch Count

154w X 196h in stitches

Design Size

11¼w X 14¼h inches on 14-count fabric

Add 4–6 inches to each measurement for cut fabric size.

DMC	X	¼	½	BS	Str	FK
310	■	▪		◢		●
400	⬆	⬆		◢		●
407	◭					
451	✖	✗				
452	⬭	⬭				
470	⊥					
472	⊞					
535	◆	◆				
543	T	T				
564	◇					
580	♣					
598	▨	▨				
676	❭			◥		
676*	∩					
742	★					
776	Z					
792	⬕					

DMC	X	¼	½	BS	Str	FK
839	⬓	⬓		◥	◥	●
841	▣	▣				
842	H	H				
922	➕					
950	V					
958	⦿					
3064	⧺	⧺				
3325	△					
3328	♥					
3340	⋔					
3706	4					
3743	⊥	⊥				
3747	L					
3827	⊘					
Blanc	▢	▢				
3790 451 }	◩	◩				

* Use 1 strand for Cross Stitch.

Top left | Top right

Bottom left | Bottom right

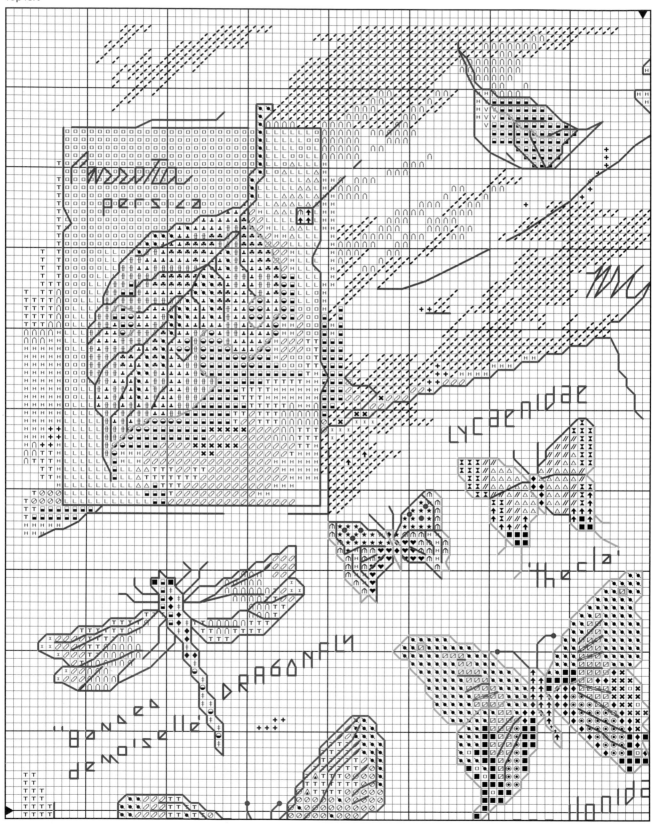

Greyed stitches indicate last row from previous section of design.

Greyed stitches indicate last row from previous section of design.

Eastern
Blue Jay

"Coleus
Croceus"

Moonlit Cranes

Design Information

Design stitched on 14-count black Aida using 3 strands for Full and ¼ Cross Stitch, 1 & 2 strands for Straight Stitch, 1 & 2 strands for Backstitch, and 1 strand for French Knots.

Blends

2 strands *E3852 and 2 strands 420
2 strands *E3852 and 2 strands 646
2 strands *E3852 and 2 strands 676
2 strands *E3852 and 2 strands 729
2 strands *E3852 and 2 strands 844
2 strands *E5270 and 2 strands 920
2 strands *E3852 and 2 strands 3823
* DMC Light Effects

Stitch Count

139w X 252h in stitches

Design Size

10⅛w X 18¼h inches on 14-count fabric

Add 4–6 inches to each measurement for cut fabric size.

DMC	X	¼	BS	Str	FK	DMC	X	¼	BS	Str	FK
211						3371					
310					●	3807					
340						3856					
402						Blanc					
420						E3852**					
436						3777					
612						E3852 } 420					
646						E3852 } 646					
647						E3852 } 676					
838						E3852 } 729					
839						E3852 } 844					
840						E5270 } 920					
844						E3852 } 3823					
898											
920											
975											
3024**											
3051											
3052					●						

** Use 2 strands for Backstitch and Straight Stitch.

Top left — Top right
Center left — Center right
Bottom left — Bottom right

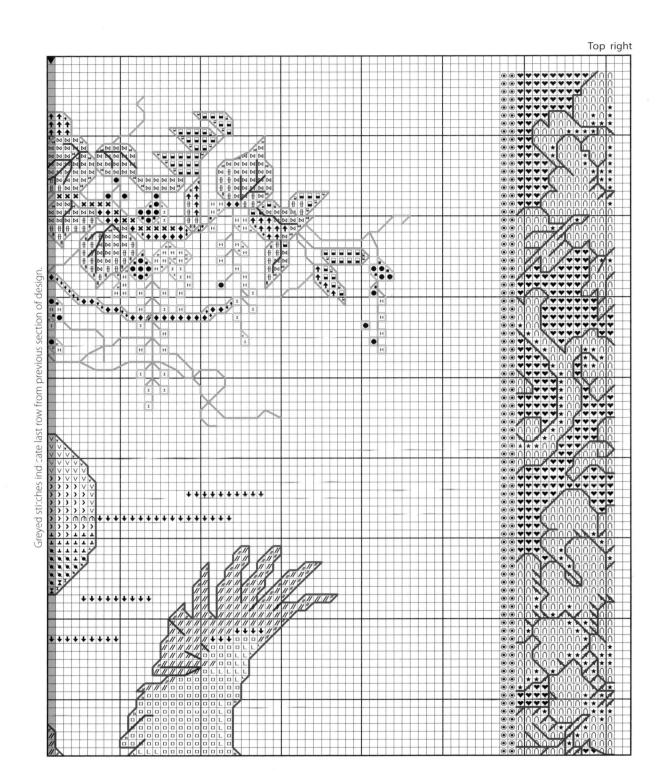

Greyed stitches indicate last row from previous section of design.

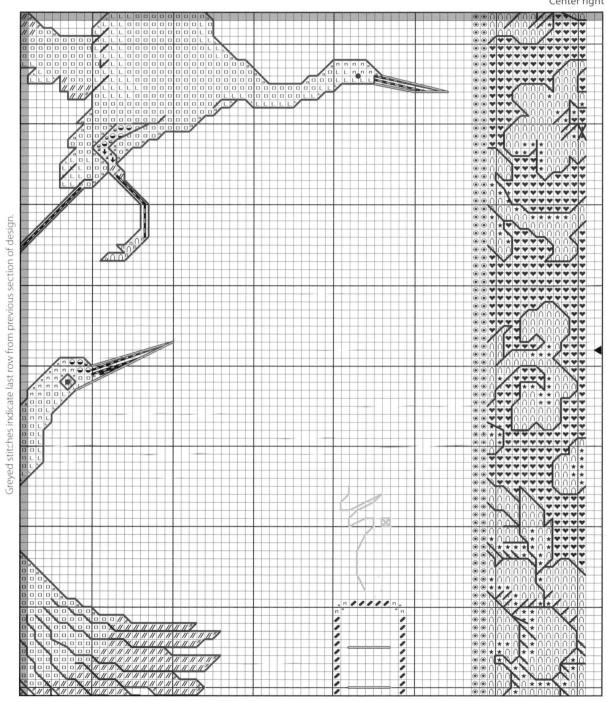

Greyed stitches indicate last row from previous section of design.

Personalization line (Do not stitch.)

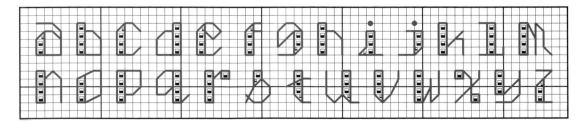

Greyed stitches indicate last row from previous section of design.

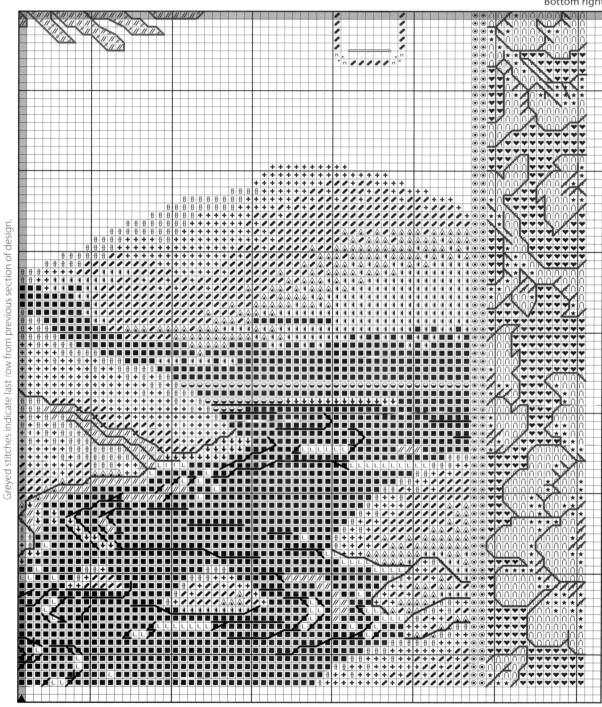

Personalization line (Do not stitch.)

A Moment of
Tranquility

Design Information

Design stitched on 14-count beige Aida using 1 & 3 strands for Full and ¼ Cross Stitch, 1 strand for ½ Cross Stitch, 1 strand for Backstitch, and 1 strand for French Knots.

Blends

1 strand 304 and 2 strands 209
1 strand 722 and 2 strands 402
1 strand 839 and 2 strands 3041

Stitch Count

154w X 196h in stitches

Design Size

11¼w X 14¼h inches on 14-count fabric

Add 4–6 inches to each measurement for cut fabric size.

DMC	X	¼	½	BS	FK
211	L	L			
224	V	V			
301	♠	♠			
356*	◆	◆		╱	
369*		□	□		
436	✚	✚			
503*	✕	✕			
504*	●	●	●		●
640				╱	
647	◖	◖		╱	
722	♥	♥			
743	◇	◇			
745	I	I			
775	✛	✛			
793*	✖				
818	H	H			
839	■	■			
932*	⊙				
977	⋂	⋂			

DMC	X	¼	½	BS	FK
3024	❱	❱			
3033	⊘	⊘			
3041*	◣	◣			╱
3064	⋔	⋔			
3752	⊘	⊘			
3770	T	T			
3776	⊥	⊥			
3856	⊟	⊟			
3863*	▼	▼			
3864*	◢	◢		╱	
3864	‡	‡			
Blanc	□	□			
304 } 209	▲	▲			
722 } 402	4	4			
839 } 3041	↑	↑			

* Use 1 strand for Full and ¼ Cross Stitch.

Top left · Top right

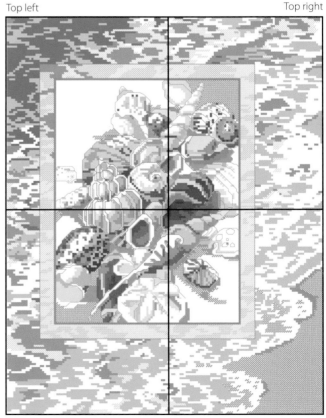

Bottom left · Bottom right

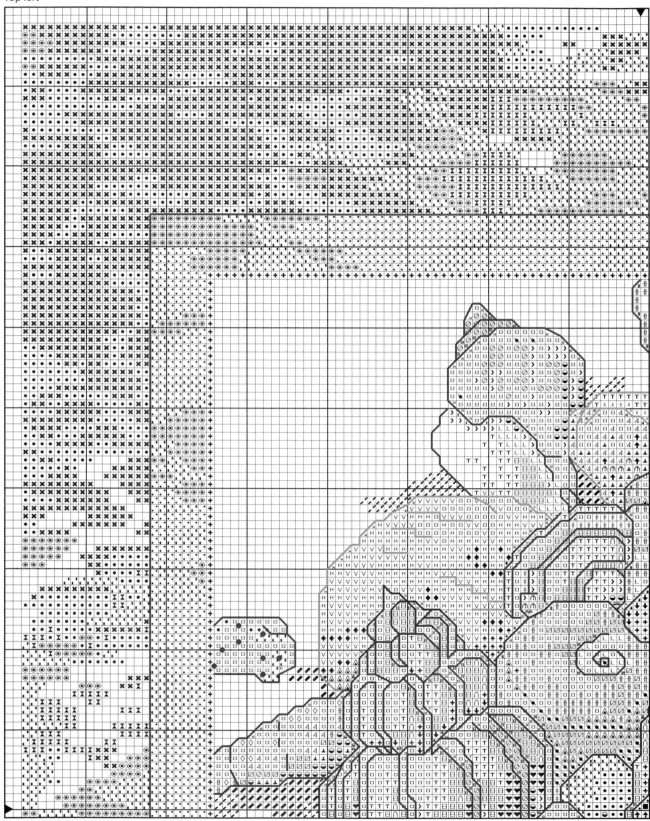

Greyed stitches indicate last row from previous section of design.

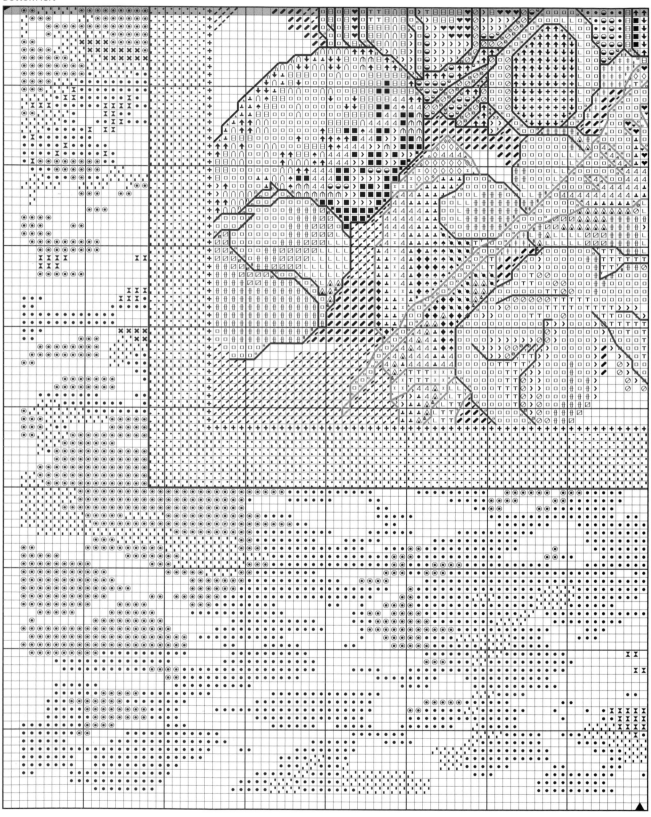

Greyed stitches indicate last row from previous section of design.

Around the
Pointe

Design Information

Design stitched on 14-count beige Aida using 3 strands for Cross Stitch, 1 & 2 strands for Backstitch, 1 & 2 strands for Straight Stitch, and 1 strand for French Knots.

Stitch Count

154w X 196h in stitches

Design Size

11¼w X 14¼h inches on 14-count fabric

Blend

1 strand 739 and 2 strands 746

Add 4–6 inches to each measurement for cut fabric size.

DMC	X	¼	BS	Str	FK
301	✚	†			
317	◖		╱		
318	⋒	⋒			
341	❭				
350*	♥		╱	╱	
415	⋈				
436	⊠	⊺	╱	╱	
436*				╱	
451	◩	◤			
453	‡				
504	⊟				
580	⬇				
722	⋒				
739	Z	ᶻ			
746	L				
747	V				
762	4	⁴			
792	●				

DMC	X	¼	BS	Str	FK
793	∕∕				
800	⊥				
839	⬆				
898	⊙		╱		●
920*	◆				
932	◇				
3042	⊡				
3348	⊞				
3743	★				
3747	H				
3776	╱	╱			
3799	■	◪	╱	╱	
3799*				╱	
3815	⊥	ᵀ			
3827	a	ᵃ			
Blanc	⊡	▫			
739 746 }	T				

* Use 2 strands for Straight Stitch and Backstitch.

Top left   Top right

Bottom left   Bottom right

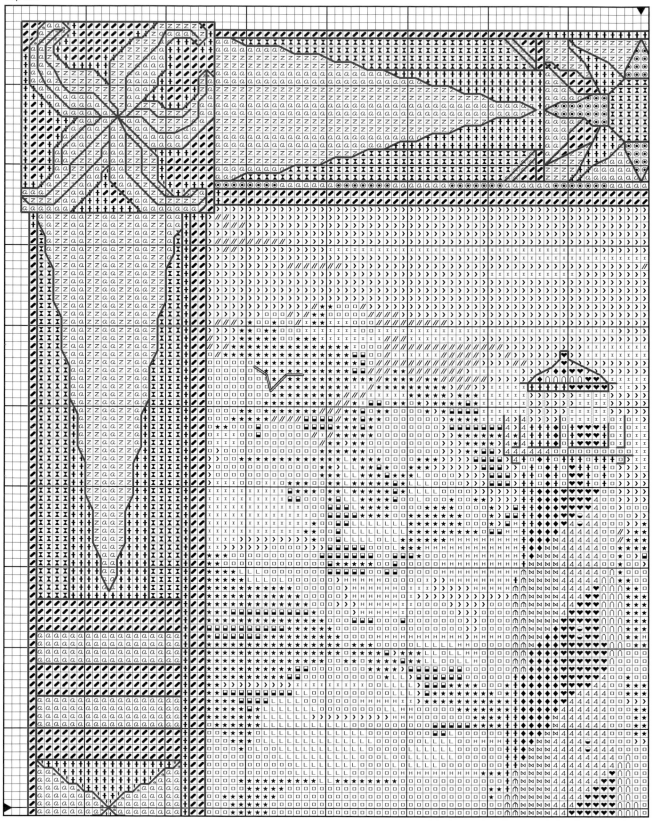

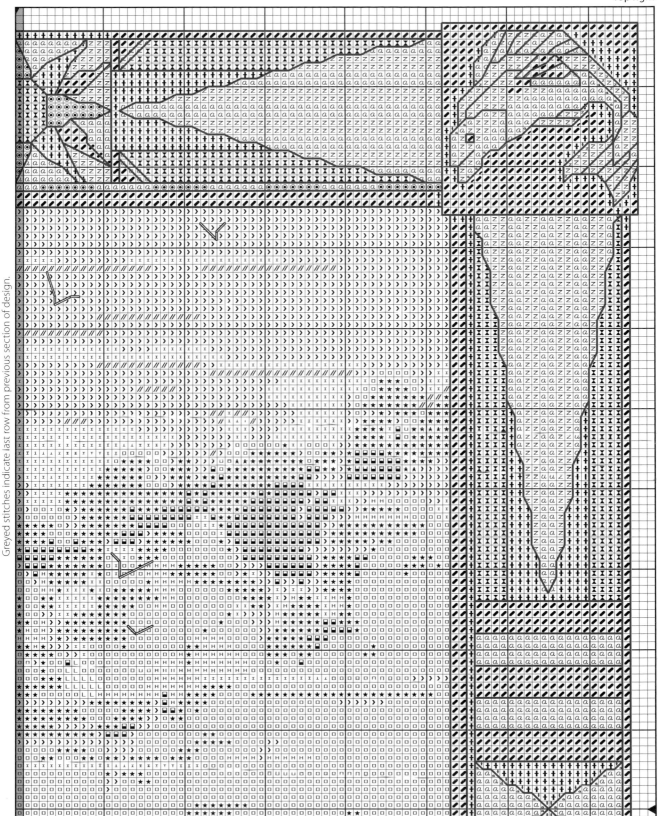

Greyed stitches indicate last row from previous section of design.

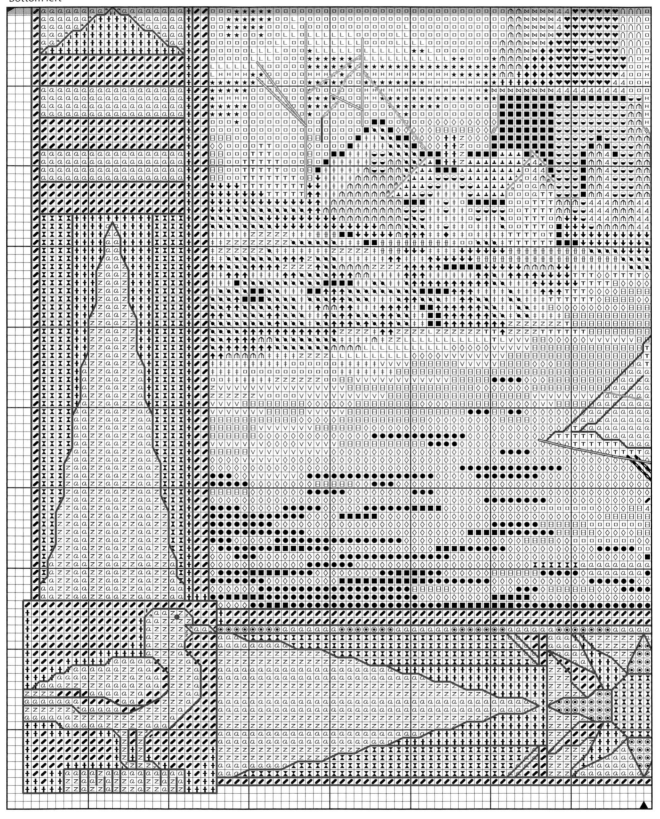

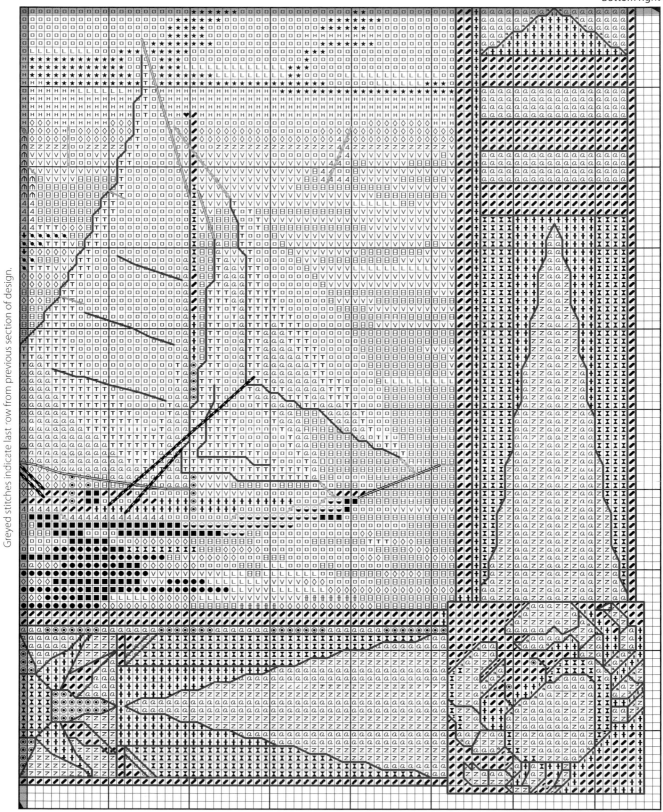

Greyed stitches indicate last row from previous section of design.

Dedication

This book is dedicated to Priscilla Timm, our technical editor and needlework expert extraordinaire. It is no exaggeration to say that every needlework design and chart created at Kooler Design Studio has benefited from the keen eye of Priscilla. Her knowledge of the needle arts, her meticulous attention to detail, and her generosity of spirit have established her as an irreplaceable member of the Kooler Design Studio team.

Acknowledgments

Thanks and appreciation to Priscilla Timm, Sandy Yarmolich and Dianne Woods for their talent and expertise, working so well together to make this book the best it could be. To our additional team members: Marsha Hinkson, Leah Travers, Mark Hanner, Jennifer Drake, and Linnea Lion for their commitment and contributions.

Many thanks to Rick Barton, Susan Sullivan, and the Leisure Arts team for their continued support and collaboration. And special thanks to Linda Gillum, Barbara Baatz Hillman, Sandy Orton and Nancy Rossi for sharing their infinite talent with us and the needlework world… what a gift that is.

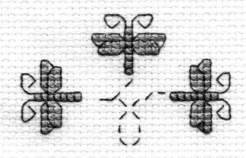